Reality & Illusion:

An Overview of Course Metaphysics

Robert Perry

Book #25 in a Series of Commentaries on *A Course in Miracles*®

THE CIRCLE OF ATONEMENT

This is the 25th book in a series, each of which deals with a particular theme from the modern spiritual teaching, *A Course in Miracles*®. The books assume a familiarity with the Course, although they might be of benefit even if you have no acquaintance with the Course. If you would like a complete listing of these books and our other publications, a sample copy of our newsletter, or information about The Circle of Atonement, please contact us at the address below.

The Circle of Atonement
Teaching and Healing Center
P.O. Box 4238, West Sedona, AZ 86340
(928) 282-0790, Fax (928) 282-0523
E-mail: info@circleofa.com
Website: www.circleofa.com

The ideas presented herein are the personal interpretation and understanding of the author, and are not necessarily endorsed by the copyright holder of A *Course in Miracles*: Foundation for *A Course in Miracles*, 41397 Buecking Dr., Temecula, CA 92590. Portions from *A Course in Miracles*, © 1996, *Psychotherapy: Purpose, Process and Practice*, and *Song of Prayer*, © 1996, reprinted by permission of the copyright holder.

All references are given for the Second Edition of the Course, and are listed according to the numbering in the Course, rather than according to page numbers. Each reference begins with a letter, which denotes the particular volume or section of the Course and its extensions (T=Text, W=Workbook for Students, M=Manual for Teachers, C=Clarification of Terms, P=Psychotherapy, and S=Song of Prayer). After this letter comes a series of numbers, which differ from volume to volume:

T, P, or S-chapter.section.paragraph:sentence; e.g., T-24.VI.2:3-4.
W-part (I or II).lesson.paragraph:sentence; e.g., W-pI.182.4:1-2.
M or C-section.paragraph:sentence; e.g., C-2.5:2.

Copyright © 1993 by The Circle of Atonement

Second Printing 2002

This is a combined reprint of two earlier booklets: *Reality & Illusion Part I*, and *Reality & Illusion Part II*.

All rights reserved

ISBN 1-886602-19-0

Cover by Kathy Simes
Layout & design by Mike Jung

Published by The Circle of Atonement: Teaching and Healing Center
Printed in the United States of America

CONTENTS

Introduction

Nothing real can be threatened.
Nothing unreal exists.
Herein lies the peace of God.

> This is how *A Course in Miracles* begins. It makes a fundamental distinction between the real and the unreal. (Preface, p. X)

As the above passage indicates (written, incidentally, by the author of the Course), the backbone of the entire Course is a razor-sharp distinction between reality and illusion. On the one side is everything positive: life, light, love, oneness, joy, peace, knowledge, God. On the other side is everything negative: death, darkness, fear, separateness, pain, ignorance, ego. And they have nothing in common: "What can be between illusion and the truth? A middle ground...must be a dream and cannot be the truth" (T-28.V.3:10-11). One side is everything; the other, pure nothingness.

From what I can see, there are two basic ways of seeking to be totally life-affirming. The first way is where you affirm literally everything: every event, every form, every thought, every feeling. No matter how dark or despicable something may look, you affirm that it must have had a hidden purpose, a camouflaged goodness, a positive reason for being, which in the end makes it worthy of love and acceptance. The Course dabbles in this view to a certain extent, in saying that every trial in this world is a lesson, and that every event, though mainly contrived by the ego, still somehow has the hand of the Holy Spirit in it.

Yet the foundation of the Course is in the second way. This way says that to be totally life-affirming, you must affirm only that which is itself absolutely life-affirming. Anything with the slightest degree of life-negation, you must negate; *not* by hating it or condemning it, but simply by denying that it really exists.

This second way is quite a bit more challenging. And it can seem far less affirming, for in the end it has to negate everything in this world.

Yet, I believe, its affirmation ends up being far more profound. For if you affirm that which limits, fragments, tortures and kills life, then your "accepting," "embracing," "inclusive" view is actually quite life-negating.

The fundamental distinction between reality and illusion is the liberating, life-affirming basis of *A Course in Miracles*. Every practical method or idea that it provides is simply an application of this basic distinction. The better we can grasp reality and illusion, then, the more effectively we can practice the path of the Course.

This book, therefore, is my attempt to communicate my current understanding of this topic. The book is not about practical application, but it *is* about the *basis* for all practical application. And, unlike the other books and booklets in this series, it is meant to be understandable to anyone, including those new to the Course. My hope, however, is that it will help clarify things even for long-time students.

PART I

Chapter 1
Common Sense Reality

Before we dive into the Course's view of reality, we need to acquaint ourselves with our normal picture of things. This will serve as a kind of baseline against which to appreciate what the Course is teaching. For this purpose, I do not want to consider "reality" from a scientific or philosophical standpoint. I merely hope to elucidate the common sense picture of reality that we all carry around. And not what we consciously or formally believe; what we act on.

I should warn you that this chapter will end up giving the world a pretty negative cast. My reasons for this are two-fold. First, I am trying to reproduce as closely as I can the Course's tone about the world. Second, how we evaluate the world depends entirely on our standard of measurement. Because most of us have no experience of anything but the world, our standard of measurement usually *is* the world. We accept its laws as a given, as reality. We do not question its limitations. We are in the condition that the Course describes when it says: "You do not ask too much of life, but far too little" (W-pI.133.2:1). Yet I believe (as I think the Course implies) that the standard of measurement that is actually native to our minds is infinity, limitlessness. No matter how much we may try to placate ourselves, we will never be satisfied with less than everything. And so, I believe, that must be the standard by which we measure the world.

Space

The first component of common sense reality to consider is *space*, for reality seems to take place inside of space. Regardless of how space should be technically described, we all have some basic, experiential sense of what it is. Space is a kind of big, empty container, a vast emptiness inside of which things exist.

This emptiness, however, has a particular structure to it. It is composed of an infinity of separate locations, separate points. Each point is separated from all other points by some kind of distance, be that distance microns or light years. To each "here" everything else must be a "there." Space is separateness carried out to the most minute level. Even at the subatomic level there is division; there is a "here" as distinct from "there."

The contents of this big, empty container are, of course, physical forms, those forms being the only thing that one sees within space. Due to the structure of space itself, all physical forms have three very important characteristics.

First, all forms are *separate*; each object exists independently of every other object. Visually, space presents us with a bewilderingly complex array of things, large, small, long, short, fat, thin, round, square, flat; all of them separated from each other by distance, all of them able to draw closer or to move apart. There is, as the Course says, "a space between all things, between all things and you" (W-pI.184.2:2).

> Look at the world, and you will see nothing attached to anything beyond itself. All seeming entities can come a little nearer, or go a little farther off, but cannot join. (T-26.I.1:7-8)

The second characteristic of physical forms is that they are all *limited*. Each one takes up a limited amount of space. Like the points in space themselves, each form is a relatively tiny "here" surrounded by an immense, seemingly endless "there."

The third characteristic of forms is that they are largely *the effect* of their environment. All forms are initially produced by forms, laws, and forces outside themselves. Thereafter, all of them are dramatically affected by outside forms, laws, and forces, and eventually these same outer factors disintegrate them.

Time

Just like space, time is also such a constant, all-pervading part of our experience, that very little description of it is needed. Just as space is the container of physical forms, time is the container of events and change.

As we all know, time is a single line along which things happen. Along this timeline are strung moments, like beads on a string. Each moment is different from every other moment, a different instant in time. In each moment, particular events happen. A moment in time, then, is a container of events, just as a location in space is a container of forms.

Time itself crawls along this line in one direction, from past to present to future. As a result, at any given time only one moment of the timeline will be present, will be alive, happening. The other moments will have either already happened and will thus be past, or will have not yet happened and will still be in the future. Time can be likened to a river, flowing in one direction along a line. Someone rafting down this river will only experience certain scenery at any given moment, the rest of the scenery being either behind him or ahead of him.

Due to the nature of time, there are three additional characteristics of everything that resides within time and space.

First, everything in time is constantly *changing*. Nothing is quite the same from one moment to the next. Just as the rafter on the river cannot stay in the same place and keep viewing the same scenery, so a being in time cannot remain the same. He will inevitably change as the river of time sweeps him forward.

Second, everything in time is *temporary*. Just as any object must occupy a limited area in space, so it must also occupy a limited amount of time. Everything, then, has a beginning and an end, a birth and a death.

Third, everything in time is largely the *product of history*. What happens in the present moment is a product of all that came before this moment. Thus, the current state of any physical form is a product of all that it has done in the past and all that has been done to it.

The Individual

As we have seen, the structure of space and time defines everything within them. And this must include ourselves, if we are truly within them. What contains us defines us. What we are is a direct product of the reality we live within. We appear to be residents of space and time, and that defines us in very fundamental ways.

As citizens of space and time, we are *separate* individuals, isolated entities separated from everything else and surrounded by a much larger environment. Therefore, we are *limited*, being no more than tiny specks in a vast expanse. We are also constantly *changing*, shifting to and fro as the winds within us and without us blow in ever-changing directions. And we are *temporary*. We have a beginning, and after our allotted three score and ten, we will inevitably have an ending.

As tiny specks in a larger environment, dwellers in one moment preceded by countless other moments, we are largely determined by forces outside of us. We are the effect of our environment, the product of our history. Our heredity, our upbringing, our schooling, our friends, our culture, have all significantly determined our specific characteristics as individuals. We are like a boulder that has been tumbled down a stream and into a river. With each rock that we bump into and each rush of water over our surface, our shape is changed to some degree. Finally, we end up at the sea as a pebble. We are the product of history and environment.

We human beings are somewhat unique specimens in time and space. For we are not just particular physical forms—bodies; we also are *minds*. And these minds have a very strange relationship with the physical world. They are, in short, in a state of fundamental conflict with the limitations of space and time. They grate against all of the characteristics of physical reality, against being separate, limited, changing, temporary effects of history and environment. As minds, we want to be free to be who we *choose* to be, not who our environment and history have decreed us to be. We are constantly trying to overcome separation and congregate in pairs, families, and social groupings. We do not want to be just one little speck; we would prefer to have everything and be everything. We want the security of permanence rather than ceaseless change. And perhaps more than anything else, we wish to break the bonds of time and last forever.

Yet, our minds not only live inside time and space, they are firmly planted inside of physical bodies. We are so contained within these bodies that we can't get out. We are trapped in them. Whatever happens to them, we have to feel. Whatever injuries they sustain, we have to suffer. They, in fact, are our only contact with the world outside of our minds. We can only perceive our world through their senses. We can only affect our world through their muscles and limbs.

These bodies enforce on us in the strictest and most immediate ways the limitations of space and time. Because they are separate, they seem to wall us off from other minds. They are limited and changing, and so we too seem to be tiny islands in constant flux. Their death places on our own selves the stamp of mortality and impermanence. Our bodies are our most immediate environment, and thus we are largely their effect. Their shape, their appearance, their sex, their age, make up an enormous part of our identities. We are largely the product of their history, of what they do and what is done to them, of their processes of eating and sleeping, growing up and aging, getting sick and recovering.

Our minds, then, are in conflict with the body's limitations. Yet this is only one example of our real conflict: our conflict with physical reality at large. For at every point the world seems to want to thwart our minds' desires and aspirations. It fired the first shot by giving birth to us as beings that are inherently lacking and needy. Both our bodies and minds are saturated with needs that must be fulfilled from outside of us. We, then, must answer this challenge and take from the world to satisfy our needs. We must eat its plants and animals. And we must take emotionally from our fellow humans. We must also defend ourselves, for the world is constantly trying to take from us, to outwit us in the struggle for the same limited resources. And so, as we try to build some sort of life, to accumulate some kind of happiness, we are constantly battling against forces that threaten to take it all away. Our whole life is a struggle against opposing forces. It is a struggle we must ultimately lose, for eventually our life will be snuffed out by death. In the end, the world must win.

If we stand back a bit, we will see this struggle being waged by every individual in time and space, inevitably pitting them all against each other. Thus, the big picture is one in which the separate pieces just do not go together. Rather than a picture of harmonious cohesiveness, it is a chaotic free-for-all in which all things are struggling against all other things. It is a picture of countless separate wills striving against each other and against the whole, against the massive forces that oppose their happiness and their very life. They find happiness here and there, but it is delicate and fleeting. They join together in alliances, but these are fragile and too often break apart. As Darwin observed, more than anything else this world is characterized by the competition for survival, by chaotic and universal conflict. As Buddha observed, life is suffering.

Chapter 2
Reality

The preceding chapter was a necessary background to give us a point of reference for appreciating what the Course is teaching. But that was its only value. For what the Course claims is that nothing we talked about in the last chapter is actually true. From its standpoint, reality as we know it is totally unreal, and, further, bears no resemblance to actual reality. In other words, the basic structure of our reality is completely false. Reality is not a realm of time and space, a place where things happen and where things exist separate and distinct from each other. And we are not limited, separate, temporary, changing body-minds who are the effects of our history and environment. You could say that reality is the complete opposite of all that. Yet even that would not fully capture what the Course is saying, for to be opposites, two things must be of a like kind. Rather than opposite, it would be more accurate to say that our current "reality" and true reality are simply and completely unrelated.

In the next two chapters we are going to do a quick overview of what the Course says about reality. Yet this overview will necessarily be tricky business, because, as mystics throughout time have emphasized, reality is indescribable. The Course reiterates this many times. It tells us that not only is it impossible for us to describe reality, but that it is literally impossible for us to understand reality as long as we are in this world: "It would indeed be impossible to be in the world with this knowledge" (T-13.VIII.1:4). "To no one here is this describable. Nor is there any way to learn what this condition means. Not till you go past learning to the Given..." (T-24.VII.6:8-10).

According to the Course, we cannot understand reality because we have placed our minds in a condition of specificity, of concreteness. Hence, we can no longer comprehend all-encompassing wholeness, but can only grasp one thing at a time. "The mind that taught itself to think specifically can no longer grasp abstraction in the sense that it is all-encompassing" (W-pI.161.4:7). Yet, given this limit on language and conceptualization, we still can glean some vague hints of what reality is like.

Infinity

Reality is not a realm of space. Rather than "space," we might speak of it as "infinity." By "infinity," I do not mean to merely suggest that reality has no boundary around it. It is more than that. Every point in reality is infinite. There are no boundaries anywhere within it, for boundaries are limits and thus clash with the idea of infinity.

Infinity is therefore not broken up into different locations as is space. There are no separate points. There is no distance. There is no "here" as opposed to "there." There is only one point, but this point has no boundaries. Reality, then, is a single, boundless "Here."

This is very difficult to describe, and is, in fact incomprehensible to our current state of mind. Perhaps the best visual symbol for reality would be an endless expanse of pure, undifferentiated light, a light that has no boundary around it and no divisions within it. The Course employs a beautiful version of this metaphor at one point:

> Beyond the body, beyond the sun and stars, past everything you see and yet somehow familiar, is an arc of golden light that stretches as you look into a great and shining circle. And all the circle fills with light before your eyes. The edges of the circle disappear, and what is in it is no longer contained at all. The light expands and covers everything, extending to infinity forever shining and with no break or limit anywhere. Within it everything is joined in perfect continuity. Nor is it possible to imagine that anything could be outside, for there is nowhere that this light is not. (T-21.I.8)

Reality, then, is not filled with physical forms. In fact, there are no forms at all, no form of any kind. The Course speaks of "the eternal formlessness of God" (C-6.5:8).

There being no forms, there are no separate things, no isolated beings, no individuals:

> To be alone is to be separated from infinity, but how can this be if infinity has no end? No one can be beyond the limitless, because what has no limits must be everywhere. (T-11.I.2:1-2)

Rather than separateness, reality is characterized by pure oneness, by oneness so complete that there is no distinction between this thing and that thing. There is only the One.

> Heaven is not a place nor a condition. It is merely an awareness of perfect Oneness, and the knowledge that there is nothing else; nothing outside this Oneness, and nothing else within. (T-18.VI.1:5-6)

Without forms, boundaries, and separateness, there can be no limitation. Reality is not filled with shades of gray, with degrees and partiality, for that is a picture of limitation. Reality is not composed of separate individuals surrounded by a larger environment, for that also is a picture of limitation.

> There is nothing outside you. That is what you must ultimately learn, for it is the realization that the Kingdom of Heaven is restored to you. (T-18.VI.1:1-2)

Therefore, things in reality are not the effect of their environment. For there literally is no environment.

Eternity

Just as there is no space in reality, so there is no time. Reality is the realm of eternity. And just as infinity is not simply endless space, but something categorically different, so eternity is not endless time. As Paul Tillich once said, a limitless stretch of linear time would be hell, not Heaven.

Time, as we saw, is a string of different moments. Eternity, however, contains only one moment. "Eternity is one time, its only dimension being 'always'" (T-9.VI.7:1). And just like the one point of infinity, the one instant of eternity is boundless. It is not like the tiny, limited moments that we experience; it is infinite.

Also unlike the moments of time, the one instant of eternity never passes away. Thus, in eternity there can be no past or future, no time that has passed nor time yet to come. The Course speaks of "one-dimensional time, proceeding from past to future," and then adds, "No one who believes this can understand what 'always' means" (T-13.I.8:3-4). Therefore, though time moves in one direction, eternity does not go anywhere. In a play on words, the Course says that "Always [all ways] has no direction" (T-13.I.3:4).

Since there is only one moment, there is no time for anything to happen in. Thus, in eternity, there are no events, no occurrences, no movement, no motion. "There is no variation. There is no interruption. There is a sense of peace so deep that no dream in this world has ever brought even a dim imagining of what it is" (T-13.XI.3:11-13).

Given all this, eternity reverses the three characteristics of things in time. In eternity, there is no change. It is pure constancy, absolute uniformity. In eternity there is nothing temporary. There are no beginnings or endings. Nothing is born and nothing will ever die. We will see in the next chapter that God creates extensions of Himself, but this does not mean that He came before them in time: "It must be understood that the word 'first' as applied to Him is not a time concept" (T-7.I.7:4). And just as nothing in infinity is the product of environment—since there is no environment—so nothing in eternity is the product of history. For there is no history.

No Individuality

If reality is spaceless and timeless, then there can be no such thing as an individual, a separate being surrounded by a larger environment. In reality there is no such animal. As we will see in the next chapter, reality contains some faint trace of individuality in the idea of "parts," but it is an individuality that bears almost no relation to how we understand the term.

And so in reality we are not separate, limited things that are constantly changing, being born and passing away. There is nothing outside of us, and so we are not at the mercy of external forces. No outside forces shape us, attack us, injure us or kill us. We are not the products of our past history, for there is no past.

In reality we do not have bodies, for bodies are physical forms and reality has no form. Thus we are not contained inside of fleshy walls, having our only contact with the outside world through the eyes and hands of those walls. Our identity is not defined by our bodily condition and appearance, nor are we at the mercy of bodily processes.

In reality our minds, being not confined to a body, are not limited. They reach out freely in all directions. They simply shine, unimpeded, unsurrounded, unbounded, unafraid. They do not use bodily senses to perceive the outer world, since there is no outer world. And so they know all of reality in direct, unmediated experience, for the knower and the known are one and the same. There is no separation of subject and object. Thus, there is no room for perception, interpretation, ambiguity and uncertainty. "In the Kingdom there is no teaching or learning, because there is no belief. There is only certainty" (T-7.II.3:4-5).

Reality is limitless mind. It is imperishable, unshakable, unqualified spirit, without form or levels, without boundaries or limits. In infinity, mind is not limited by an outer reality; mind *is* reality. It is therefore utterly free: "spirit is eternally free" (T-1.IV.2:8). It cannot conflict with anything. There is nothing to oppose it, to confine it, to thwart its desires, or to kill it. In reality, mind is not in conflict with anything, for it is everything. "Reality is everything, and you have everything because you are real" (T-9.I.13:3).

Reality, therefore, has precisely zero in common with the fundamental structure of time and space. There is no overlap whatsoever. Unlike time and space, reality has no different locations nor different moments. And while the separate parts that live inside time and space do not go together, being in a state of perpetual conflict, reality is wholly different. Its parts—if we can even speak of parts—go together with perfect harmony, for they are one. Therefore, reality is not characterized by chaos, conflict, competition, and strife. It is pervaded by serene oneness. And whereas the world is filled with suffering, reality contains no pain or suffering of any kind, not even the slightest lack. There is only unbounded joy.

Pain is illusion; joy, reality. Pain is but sleep; joy is awakening. Pain is deception; joy alone is truth.

(W-pI.190.10:4-6)

Chapter 3
Heaven

The preceding chapter was meant to be a somewhat technical discussion of reality, providing the basic shape of infinity/eternity. Yet, although the Course uses the technical language that we have used above, its emphasis is on what you could call more personal language. Reality, in its vocabulary, is synonymous with Heaven. Heaven is the dwelling place of a Divine Father and Son, Who live in an intimate relationship of perfect love. In this chapter, we will examine Heaven as the Course portrays it.

God

In truth, the Course's view of Heaven—and reality—begins with God. To my mind, the Course is as profoundly God-centered as a teaching could be. In one of my favorite passages about God, it tells us:

> The first in time means nothing, but the First in eternity is God the Father, Who is both First and One. Beyond the First there is no other, for there is no order, no second or third, and nothing but the First. (T-14.IV.1:7-8)

Where does one begin in talking about God? Perhaps the best description of God would be just a hallowed silence. As the Course says at one point, "We say, 'God is,' and then we cease to speak, for in that knowledge words are meaningless" (W-pI.169.5:4). As this passage suggests, words cannot remotely capture Who or What God is. Yet we can say some things that will send our minds in the right direction, before they, too, fall short.

Being part of reality, God would have to have the characteristics of reality that were described in the previous chapter. He would have to be infinite and eternal, rather than separate, limited, changing, and temporary. Further, being God, He must be dependent for His existence on nothing. He is not the creation of some other creator, the effect of another cause. He is the uncreated Creator, the uncaused Cause. He is also not a part of some larger domain, not a being inside a larger matrix. He is the Matrix itself. In other words, He is not surrounded by space of any kind. Strictly speaking, rather than being a part of reality, He is reality itself, its Container and its Content.

In contrast to a modern tendency to bring Heaven down off of its "unrealistic" heights—to view God as imperfect and changing, and to gravitate toward a more earth-centered spirituality—the Course goes in the opposite direction. If you could take the positive notions of God that you have inherited from Western spirituality—of a God that is loving, merciful, wise, just—and then elevate, expand, and purify those concepts to the highest possible degree, and send them out into infinity, far, far beyond where your limited mind can go, you would have some distant notion of the God of the Course.

To my mind, the keynote of the God of the Course is just that. In Him, all truly positive qualities are absolute, or, as the Course says, *maximal*. God, then, is holiness, love, peace, joy, power, knowledge—all raised to a maximal level.

Positive qualities in a maximal state: that may not sound very impressive at first blush, but let us reflect on it further. What does it imply? To begin with, it implies that those qualities would have to be without limit. There could be no limit to God's joy, for instance. Were it limited, it would not be maximal. All of God's qualities, then, are unlimited, infinite. Also, without limit implies without form, for all form is limited. God's qualities are formless.

Maximal also implies that these qualities would have to be more than mere attributes that God possesses. For to possess something implies a separation or distinction between the possessor and the possession. And a love that is simply a possession would not be as maximal as a love that one *is*. Therefore, God does not have love; He *is* love. He is the pure spirit of love itself. As the Course points out many times, in Heaven there is no difference between having and being.

Maximal also implies without change or fluctuation. Normally, we think of a person's qualities being in a constant state of flux. He is loving one moment, not so loving the next; peaceful one moment, disturbed the next. This is just how God is described in the Bible; He changes His Mind and experiences changing emotions. Yet fluctuation implies highs and lows, the lows being necessarily less than maximal. Therefore, it would be impossible for God to fluctuate, since He is always maximal. As the Course says, "Nor is it possible to love... totally at times. You cannot be totally committed sometimes" (T-7.VII.1:3-4). God would therefore be pure, motionless Mind, unqualified Spirit, resting in perfect stillness and quiet.

A maximal quality would be one without different kinds or levels. There could not be different kinds of love, for instance, or different levels of love. For, necessarily, some kinds and some levels would be of a lesser or weaker degree, and thus not maximal. As the Course says:

> Perhaps you think that different kinds of love are possible. Perhaps you think there is a kind of love for this, a kind for that; a way of loving one, another way of loving still another. Love is one. It has no separate parts and no degrees; no kinds nor levels, no divergencies and no distinctions. It is like itself, unchanged throughout. It never alters with a person or a circumstance. It is the Heart of God. (W-pI.127.1)

Maximal also implies that each quality would have to be unopposed by an opposite. God could not include both love and hate, both power and weakness, both joy and sadness. For love mixed with hate gets you something in the middle, resulting in a love that is not maximal. Hence, for love to be truly maximal, there must be nothing present to dilute it. God would therefore be simply incapable of even the slightest feeling that was not pure love; incapable of even a tiny hint of disapproval, anger, irritation or frustration. He could not even be aware of anything that is not love. Why? When you are *aware* of hate—even if it is not your own—the simple awareness of it means that in your own mind there is a little mental copy of the hate you see outside of you. Thus there is a little bit of hate now in your mind. And that would dilute the love inside of you, thus rendering it non-maximal.

This would be true of all of God's qualities. For instance, God would have to be so holy that He would actually not comprehend anything but the purest, most unspeakable holiness. He would not see, react to, give birth to, or allow to exist, anything that was remotely sinful or impure. The same would be true of His power. He would have to be so powerful that there could be nothing opposing His Will, nothing in the way of It. No kingdoms of evil could sneak in the back door of Heaven and battle with Him for control of reality. Only what He willed could be real and there could be absolutely nothing impeding His Will. His Will would have to be instantaneous in accomplishment, never gradual or delayed. "God does not take steps, because His accomplishments are not gradual" (T-7.I.7:1).

In fact, there would be nothing halfway about Him. Everything about Him would have to be total: undivided and unbounded. In His Mind, there would be no hint of uncertainty, indecision, or vacillation. In speaking about God, the Course is careful to use terms that do not imply ambivalence, but instead, absoluteness. In Course language, God knows; He does not perceive. For "knowing" has the connotation of direct certainty. Yet in "perceiving" there is room for uncertainty. God creates; He does not make. For "create" has a note of force and finality to it that "make" does not. God wills; He does not wish. For "no one in his right mind believes that what is wished is as real as what is willed" (T-3.VI.11:7).

The God we are sketching, this unbounded, unchanging Mind, does not sound much like a person. In fact, He would not be a person as we understand personhood, for of course a person as normally conceived is a limited being within a larger matrix. Yet, on the other hand, He would also not be an unconscious force, for in important respects that would make Him *less* than a person—less aware, less intelligent, less free. From what I see in the Course, God is *more*, rather than less, than a person in every way. For instance, He is spoken of as having all the abilities of a person—will, awareness, thought, feeling. Yet these must necessarily be raised to a maximal level, taking Him inconceivably far beyond the bounds of personhood as we think of it. With this understanding, though, I think it would be appropriate to call God a Person, using a capital "P."

And, of course, He would have no gender. In calling God "He" the Course does not mean to suggest that God is male, or even more male than female. Strictly speaking, He is not even *both* male and female. Such earthly categories do not apply to Him. From the Course's standpoint, our male and female are illusions, tiny splinters off of God's infinite qualities. Calling God "He," then, is just a convenience of language.

Speaking of language: I want to reiterate that even though I have just used quite a few words in talking about God, in actuality it is impossible to describe Him. And so, God has not just been described. The only purpose of the preceding words was to send our minds in the general direction of Something that transcends their current capacity as much as the ocean exceeds the capacity of a thimble.

Creation

God has only one "need" and thus only one "activity." "God has created...out of His need to extend His Love. With love in you, you have no need except to extend it" (T-15.V.11:2-3). The Course describes God's Love as literally so vast, so deep, so uncontainable, that it must overflow. It must give, it must share itself. Being pure love, it yearns only to give all of itself away. And so, in the stillness of eternity, God's Love shines outward, not as some kind of automatic, mindless process, but as God's Self-giving.

> To create is to love. Love extends outward simply because it cannot be contained. Being limitless it does not stop. It creates forever, but not in time. (T-7.I.3:3-6)

As the above passage implies, this extension of love is the act of creation. Thus, like the God of the Judaeo-Christian tradition, the God of the Course does create. He does express Himself in the form of new existence.

This creation, however, is quite different from creation as conceived of in the West. In our Western traditions, God's creation is separate and distinct from Him. Like a potter, His creations are fashioned by Him, yet are not inherently joined to Him. And these creatures are also separated from each other. What's more, God's creation is unlike Him. God is Spirit, yet He creates a physical universe of time and space. God is one, yet He creates an endless diversity. God is holy, yet He makes creatures that start out resembling Him—being made "in His image"—but quickly corrupt themselves into something sinful and evil.

In the Course, however, creation is conceived of in an entirely different way. It is admitted that in creation God has given birth to something "new," yet this "new" creation is at the same time still connected to God, one with God, part of God, even made of God. Creation as conceived by the Course, then, has at its center a tension between *newness* and *sameness*. In short, it is completely paradoxical.

On the level of sameness, the Course makes it clear that creation is *extension*. In that single word, a whole new vision of creation is implied. For "extension" implies that the creation remains connected to its Source, not separate. It also implies that to create it, God simply extended His Own Spirit. This implies that the creation is made of the same thing as God, made of His Substance. Thus, the creation, in a certain sense, is God; for just as a wave is made of ocean water, God's creation is made of God.

Further, this creation remains *inside* of God. Because God is not a physical being creating other physical beings, He does not create using hands. He creates by thought. His creations are simply His Thoughts. And thoughts do not leave the mind of the thinker. They have no life outside of it. They are inside of that mind, part of it, joined with it. "God placed [His Son] in Himself where pain is not, and love surrounds him without end or flaw" (T-13.VII.7:3). This is an application of one of the Course's basic principles: "Ideas leave not their source" (see, for example, W-pI.132.5:3; W-pI.167.3:6). Because we are nothing more than Thoughts in God's Mind, we are not end-products of God's creative act, as a clay pot is the product of a potter's creative act. We *are* the act. We are simply *the motion of God creating*. We are a gesture in His Mind.

Thus, the creation is the *same* as God: connected to Him, one with Him, part of Him, inside of Him, made of Him.

> God created His Sons by extending His Thought, and retaining the extension of His Thought in His Mind. All His Thoughts are thus perfectly united within themselves and with each other. (T-6.II.8:1-2)

Yet, in spite of this sameness, there still is newness. If there was nothing new, then the result of God's creating would be zilch. And the Course makes it clear dozens of times that creation has an exalted purpose and result. To draw a bead on this purpose and result, let us look again at the word "extension." Extension does imply sameness, in that it pictures a substance that is not changed, but is simply extended outward. Yet is also implies newness in that it implies an *increase*, an expansion. One of the definitions of "extend" in Webster's Dictionary is "to increase the bulk of." To say that God extends Himself is to say that God expands Himself.

Somehow in the timeless sameness of reality, God's Love overflows, extends outward, and actually expands. Even in this world, when love is shared, it grows fuller. And in some inscrutable way, it is the same in Heaven. God gives His Love, and that Love becomes more.

It takes only a little thought to realize that this newness involves us in many intellectual difficulties. How can there be anything new in changeless eternity? The Course, therefore, is quick to correct overly simplistic ways of thinking about this extension.

To begin with, we must not think that because God has extended Himself "outward" that there *is* any outward—some kind of space outside of God into which He extends.

> Mind reaches to itself....It does not go out. Within itself it has no limits, and there is nothing outside it....It encompasses you entirely; you within it and it within you. There is nothing else, anywhere or ever.
> (T-18.VI.8:5, 7-8, 10-11)

Nor does it mean that God's act of extension was an event in time. It was not a process that took place over time—we already saw that God's "accomplishments are not gradual" (T-7.I.7:1). Nor was it an event preceded by other events and followed by still other events: "God's creations have always been, because He has always been" (T-7.I.3:7).

Further, to say that God has increased does not mean that He has changed. We are told that reality "does not change by increase....If you perceive it as not increasing you do not know what it is" (T-7.I.7:10-11). In other words, expansion is an inherent part of God's nature. To be Himself—to stay the same—He must increase.

Still further, to say that extension adds more to God should not be taken in a simplistic, quantitative sense. As the Course says, "nothing is added that is different because everything has always been" (T-10.In.2:4). And it especially should not be taken to imply that He was incomplete to start with:

> True giving is creation. It extends the limitless to the unlimited, eternity to timelessness, and love unto itself. It adds to all that is complete already, not in simple terms of adding more, for that implies that it was less before. It adds by letting what cannot contain itself fulfill its aim of giving everything it has away, securing it forever for itself. (W-pI.105.4:2-5)

Thus, we are left with a paradox, something our minds simply cannot grasp. Somehow, in timelessness there are timeless events, motionless motions; which increase the unchangeable and add to the already infinitely complete.

The Son

God has only one creation. Out of God was born one timeless Thought, a Spirit as pure, as holy, as limitless, and as vast as God Himself. This creation is the Son, the Christ. The Christ is a single universal Self of unimaginable magnitude. He is one, just as God is one.

> And here, before the altar to one God, one Father, one Creator and one Thought, we stand together as one Son of God. (W-pI.187.10:2)

Although creation can be thought of as an abstract, impersonal act, the Course makes the creation of the Son sound more like a transcendental version of the love-filled conceiving of children. It was an act of love, a gift: "God gave Himself to you in your creation" (T-10.V.10:10). And once this giving occurred, the Son became God's only Love, "His one creation and His only joy" (W-pII.9.4:4), "His one creation and His happiness, forever like Himself and one with Him" (C-5.3:1). My favorite passage on God's Love comes from *The Gifts of God*, which was dictated to Helen Schucman after the Course. In this passage Jesus reaches for the most powerful examples of love in this world, to give us some dim idea of God's Love for His Son:

> He loves you as a mother loves her child; her only one, the only love she has, her all-in-all, extension of herself, as much a part of her as breath itself. He loves you as a brother loves his own; born of one father still as one in him, and bonded with a seal that cannot break. He loves you as a lover loves his own; his chosen one, his joy, his very life, the one he seeks when he has gone away, and brings him peace again on her return. He loves you as a father loves his son, without whom would his self be incomplete, whose immortality completes his own, for in him is the chain of love complete—a golden circle that will never end, a song that will be sung throughout all time and afterwards, and always will remain the deathless sound of loving and of love. (*The Gifts of God*, p. 126)

If there is a love story in the Course, it is the story of the Father and the Son. The Course never ceases to speak of the eternal Love that lies between Them. Although the Course uses such technical terms as extension, creation, and increase, its language about the Father and the Son is more often than not the language of love, suggesting both the intimacy of lovers and the deep affection of parents and children.

One of the Course's recurring metaphors for the love of the Father and the Son is that of a song, a song of love sung by Father and Son to each other: "Endless the harmony, and endless, too, the joyous concord of the Love They give forever to Each Other" (S-I.In.1:3). God sings to us a "vast song of honor and of love" that "pours from God to you eternally in loving praise of what you are" (T-24.II.4:5,4). And then we return to Him this song, "a song of gratitude and love and praise by everything created to the Source of its creation" (T-26.IV.3:5), "the ceaseless song that all creation sings unto its God" (S-2.I.8:6), "this ancient hymn of love the Son of God sings to his Father still" (T-21.I.9:6).

The relationship of Father and Son, God and Christ, Creator and created, says the Course, is the only real relationship, the true model that all relationships in this world should aspire to reflect. The giving between Father and Son is the model for all giving. Their love is the only love there is, "the only love that is fully given and fully returned. Being complete, it asks nothing. Being wholly pure, everyone joined in it has everything" (T-15.VII.1:3-5). The Course spares no praises of this relationship, which it characterizes as "wholly loving and forever...one of perfect union and unbroken continuity...wholly Self-encompassing and Self-extending" (T-20.VI.1:3,5,7).

> In this eternal, still relationship, in which communication far transcends all words, and yet exceeds in depth and height whatever words could possibly convey, is peace eternal. (W-pI.183.11:6)

At the heart of this relationship, we find the same basic paradox that we discussed under the heading of "creation," the paradox of sameness and newness. Only here it is in slightly different form. It is the paradox which the Course captures when it says, "Only God Himself is more than they [His Sons] but they are not less than He is" (T-9.VI.3:6). In other words, the Son is both equal to God and less than God.

Let us look at equality first. In creating the Son, the Course says, God gave all of Himself to the Son. He held nothing back, literally nothing. Thus the Son—which is Who we are—is equal to God. Think about that: *You* are equal to God! This is literally true—for the simple reason that God is not selfish. He shares Himself so fully that He gives all of Himself away to every one of His creations. "His glory belongs to Him, but it is equally yours. You cannot, then, be less glorious than He is" (T-9.VI.3:10-11). Because of this, says the Course, "you will never be content with being less [than God]" (T-29.VIII.9:11).

Thus, the Son shares all of God's attributes; in fact, shares all of God. And remember, what God gives remains an indissoluble part of Him. So in this sense there is absolutely no difference between Father and Son—no superiority or inferiority, no rank or hierarchy, no place where one begins and the other ends, no distinction whatsoever.

Yet, the Course says, there is *one* distinction between Father and Son: "In creation you are not in a reciprocal relation to God, since He created you but you did not create Him" (T-7.I.1:4). This, then, is the only sense in which we and God are different. He created us; we didn't create Him.

Thus, even though God is our equal, He is also our Creator. He is our God. And when we know Him face to face, He will be as close, familiar, and intimate as our own Self, for in a very real sense He is our Self. Yet we will also have another reaction to God: *awe*. For we will be the created viewing its Creator. We will be the stream looking up at its Source. This awe has nothing to do with fear. It is simply the appropriate response to Something that stands above the substance of our being. As the Course says, "a state of awe is worshipful, implying that one of a lesser order stands before his Creator" (T-1.II.3:2).

To summarize the paradox: God is *more* than us in that He created us, but we are *not less* than He is in the sense that He gave us all of Himself, making us His equals.

The Parts

As we said, the Son, the Christ, is one. Yet here again we encounter a paradox, for the Son also includes within Himself an infinite number of "parts" (also called "sons," "brothers," "children," "aspects," or "pieces"). These parts, as the Course implies countless times, are God-created. In other words, even though God created only one thing, at the same time, within that oneness He created a plurality, as the following passage implies: "Creation is the sum of all God's Thoughts, in number infinite, and everywhere without all limit" (W-pII.11.1:1).

These parts, however, are nothing like parts as we think of them in this world. When we say "part," what do we usually mean? We mean a piece, a portion, of a whole. This piece is distinct from the whole—being only *part* of it—and is also distinct from the other parts of the whole, all of which have different shapes and sizes. These parts are organized into particular relationships to produce a specific overall configuration, which we call the whole.

Parts in Heaven, however, are a whole different matter. In some sense, it seems, they are distinct from each other and from the whole. But in a more important sense, they most definitely are not:

> One brother is all brothers. Every mind contains all minds, for every mind is one. (W-pI.161.4:1-2)

> All of God's Sons are of equal value, and their equality is their oneness. The whole power of God is in every part of Him. (T-11.VI.10:5-6)

Unlike parts in this world, the parts of the Son are identical to each other. Let us explain this a step at a time. First, they are *equal* to each other. There is no hierarchy among them, no superiority or inferiority, no specialness. Yet equal things can still be different. And so, second, they are the *same* as each other. They have the exact same nature, the same needs, the same feelings. There is no difference whatsoever among the parts of the Sonship, no specialization. They have no special needs, special abilities, or special temperaments. Yet things that are the same can still be separate, like identical twins, for instance. And so, third, they are *one*, joined. They are not separate parts, but are somehow the same Thing.

Further, in total contrast to parts in this world, in Heaven each part is at the same time the whole. In other words, a part is both simply one part and is also quite literally the whole.

> In perception the whole is built up of parts that can separate and reassemble in different constellations....The idea of part-whole relationships has meaning only at the level of perception....[In knowledge or reality] there is no difference between the part and whole.
>
> (T-8.VIII.1:12,14,15)

This means that in Heaven there are no true parts in the sense that we think of them. In other words, there is nothing *partial.* "There is nothing partial about knowledge. Every aspect is whole" (T-13.VIII.2:1-2). "Every aspect *is* the whole" (T-13.VIII.5:3).

In Heaven this state is quite natural: "The recognition of the part as whole, and of the whole in every part is perfectly natural" (T-16.II.3:3). Yet in our current state of mind it is one of those paradoxical things that we truly cannot comprehend, since that state is only able to take in one thing—one part—at a time. "What can [these words] seem to be but empty sounds; pretty, perhaps, correct in sentiment, yet fundamentally not understood nor understandable" (W-p I.161.4:6).

Yet there are some good analogies for the idea that the part can be the whole. Perhaps the best analogy for this is a hologram. As many are aware, a hologram is a piece of film that contains overlapping wave patterns. When a laser beam is shone through the film, a three-dimensional image is projected. Yet, fascinatingly, when the film is cut up into pieces, each piece is able to produce the entire original three-dimensional image. Each part contains the whole. Yet, even this is only an analogy. There are no actual examples of the complete identity of part and whole in time-space, and the hologram is no exception. For when you cut up a piece of holographic film, what you get are a bunch of separate pieces that all simply contain the same information, the same wave patterns.

One last contrast between earthly parts and heavenly parts: In earthly wholes, the parts make up the whole. The whole is simply the product of them, the sum of them. If the parts are disassembled, the whole no longer exists, but the parts still exist. Yet Heaven overturns even this basic idea. In Heaven the whole is not the product of its parts: "The Sonship in its Oneness transcends the sum of its parts" (T-2.VII.6:3). It is the whole that seems to be the more primary, the more foundational. The parts are not its building blocks. They are simply aspects of a prior or preexisting whole, one that is not built out of parts. It would be more accurate, in fact, to say that the parts are products of the whole than the other way around. "The whole does define the part, but the part does not define the whole" (T-8.VIII.1:10).

Why is it so important to determine the nature of these parts? The reason is very simple: *we are the parts.*

> We are creation; we the Sons of God. We seem to be discrete, and unaware of our eternal unity with Him. Yet back of all our doubts, past all our fears, there still is certainty. (W-pII.11.4:1-3)

Beyond our seeming identities as separate, limited, temporary, changing body-minds, each one of us is a part of God's one Son, the Christ. As such we are all totally equal; none of us is superior, special. We are all completely the same; none of us is different, unusual, strange. We are all joined; none of us is separate, apart, or alone. As parts we are all brothers (or sisters—the language is unimportant), all Sons of the same Father, Daughters of the same Mother, rays from the same sun. Regardless of our seeming differences in age, skin color, intelligence, wealth, social status, "moral" character, or spiritual development, we are all the same. Even Jesus, who has traditionally been called the Christ, is only one of the parts, and as such is equal to us, the same as us, joined with us. This is why the term "Christ" in the

Course refers to all of us and does not refer to Jesus any more than anyone else.

And yet each one of us is also the whole. Each one of us is the single Self that unites us all, the Christ, the single Self that God created, "the perfect Son of God, His one creation and His happiness, forever like Himself and one with Him" (C-5.3:1).

We Are Creators

As we saw, in creating us, God gave us all of Himself. He held nothing back. "Divine Abstraction takes joy in sharing" (T-4.VII.5:4). And so, even though He could not share with us His creation of us (since that would require us to reciprocate and create Him, a logical impossibility), He could share with us the *function of creating*. In other words, He created us to be creators. "God is more than you only because He created you, but not even this would He keep from you. Therefore you can create as He did" (T-9.VI.4:1-2).

The Course mentions hundreds of times that in Heaven we are creators. We therefore have creations, who are our children just as we are God's children. These are not created apart from God nor apart from the rest of the Sonship. To create, all of the Sons of God join together as one to receive God's creative Power as it flows to us. And then in unison with each other and with God, we extend it outward. These creations, by the way, are part of God's one Son, an extension of God's Kingdom. They do not constitute another Son of God.

What are these creations? Well, it does not take a Rhodes scholar to answer that, since everything in Heaven is exactly the same. At one point the Course offers a description of both our creations and ourselves, saying that what we create must be like us:

> A perfect being, all-encompassing and all-encompassed, nothing to add and nothing taken from; not born of size nor place nor time, nor held to limits or uncertainties of any kind. (T-24.VII.7:3)

We now have discussed the "occupants" of Heaven: God, the Son and the Son's creations. Now we can turn our attention briefly to the experience of Heaven. What is Heaven like? What is it like to live there?

Extension

Though we have discussed the dynamic of extension a few times, we need to say more about it, for extension is the single dynamic of Heaven. As such it contains the key to the experience of Heaven. Extension is what everyone "does" in reality and it is what everyone experiences in reality.

To understand (as best we can) this transcendental event, this timeless motion, we should perhaps approach it in stages. In the most simple terms, to extend is to *give*. Extension is the act of a part of Heaven giving to another part—a brother giving to another brother.

Further, what is extended is not a physical form, for there are no forms in Heaven. In the Course, extension is synonymous with *communication*. Therefore, what is extended must be ideas, not physical forms.

And, as we all know, when you give ideas, you do not lose them. You still have them, even though you have given them away. Therefore, now both you, the giver, and the receiver share them. As a result, to be more accurate we must say that extension is not just giving and communicating, it is *sharing*.

To continue filling this picture out, in Heaven there is no duality of having and being. We are not beings that have certain possessions. The ideas we possess, and would communicate, are ourselves. What we extend is our own being. Therefore, extension is not just giving, communicating, sharing; it is joining.

Finally, this giving/communicating/sharing/joining must necessarily be completely nonspecific and nonselective, for that is the nature of Heaven:

> [Illusory] existence as well as [heavenly or real] being rest on communication. Existence, however, is specific in how, what and with whom communication is judged to be worth undertaking. Being is completely without these distinctions. It is a state in which the mind is in communication with everything that is real.
>
> ..."How," "what" and "to whom" are irrelevant, because real creation gives everything....In the state of being the mind gives everything always. (T-4.VII.4:1-4, 5:6,8)

In other words, in Heaven extension is total, absolutely total. You are giving all of yourself away to everything all the time. What you give is total—you give all of yourself. What you give *to* is total—you give to totality. And the time in which you do this giving is also total, since you are doing this outside of time, in eternity. The closest analogy in this world is light, which shines constantly and impartially in all directions. And this is what we are doing in Heaven: constantly, nonselectively, and without inhibition, shining out like rays from the sun, to merge with the All and to "extend the allness and the unity of God" (W-pI.95.12:2).

What is the result of extension? As we saw with God's creation of the Son, extension increases the giver, the source of the extension. Yet this does not give quite a full enough picture. When you extend, something across-the-board happens to your reality. Your reality is *confirmed*, for, unless you extend, you cannot be real: "Nothing God created but would extend....Whatever does not fulfill this function cannot be real" (T-17.IV.1:6-7). Also, your reality and nature are *revealed*: "Therefore, what extends from the mind is still in it, and from *what* it extends it knows itself" (T-6.III.1:2). Further, your reality is *maintained*: "Being *must* be extended. That is how it retains the knowledge of itself" (T-7.IX.2:6-7). "Be confident that you have never lost your Identity and the extensions which maintain It in wholeness and peace" (T-7.IX.7:1). And in addition, as we have said, your reality is actually *increased.*

Love

Having looked more closely at extension, we can see that it is really the same thing as love: "Love is extension" (T-24.I.1:1). For in love we experience the same going out of ourselves in giving, sharing, communicating, and joining. If extension is the single occupation of Heaven, and if extension is love, then Heaven is all about love. Let us take a quick look at love as we know it, and then see what it tells us about Heaven.

Think about when you love something. You are perceiving it as extremely valuable, worthy, and desirable. Because of this, you feel an attraction to it. For to see something as valuable or desirable is not just to see it as positive in itself; it is to see it as positive *in relation to you*, to see it as good for you, as compatible with you, as suiting you. Therefore, you want to join with it, to go beyond yourself and unite with it. "In every case, you join it without reservation because you love it, and would be with it. And so you rush to meet it, letting your limits melt away" (T-18.VI.12:4-5). You also want to give to it, to bless it, for since it is now your happiness, its benefit has become your benefit. What makes it shine brighter makes you shine brighter, too.

Love, then, is the experience of something so desirable, so valuable, so worthy, so *lovable*, that it draws you beyond your boundaries to give to it, join with it, and share yourself with it.

Now what the Course is saying about Heaven is that we have total, undivided, undiluted, unlimited love towards every single thing in Heaven all of the time. Think about that: Each member of Heaven is so desirable, so valuable, so good for us, so compatible with us, that we want to give all of ourselves to it always. In the one moment of eternity, then, we are simultaneously giving all of ourselves to each and every part of Heaven, as well as to the Creator of Heaven. And every part of Heaven, including its Creator, is eternally giving all of itself to us. This is the forgotten song. This, says the Course, is love, the only real love, God's Love. Nothing else is worthy of the name. "Love is extension. To withhold the smallest gift is not to know love's purpose. Love offers everything forever" (T-24.I.1:1-3).

Heaven, then, is pure embrace, all-encompassing compatibility. "It is total inclusion....perfect inclusion..." (T-6.II.6:5,10). Absolutely nothing is rejected, because rejection goes directly against the nature of love. And without rejection, there can be no selecting, evaluating, organizing or judging, for all of those require rejection in some form. In Heaven we have absolutely no critical faculty, no basis for any sifting, choosing, or discerning. We are wide open to infinity.

Everything about Heaven is summarized in the idea of love, for love is Heaven's one dynamic. It is Heaven's "*one* meaning, *one* emotion and *one* purpose" (T-14.VII.7:5). Love contains within itself every attribute of Heaven. Love is holiness, for love in itself is pure, clean and perfect, and only responds to what it sees as similarly immaculate. Love is power: It can evoke a response more powerful than any other, since only what you love are you willing to give all of your energy to. Love is knowledge, for to love is to directly know the heart of reality.

It is in this vein that we must take the Course's statement that love is the only true emotion. The Course does not mean that other positive emotions such as peace and joy do not exist. It simply means that love contains them within itself. Love is the summary emotion of reality.

For instance, love contains within itself joy, for love is a joyous feeling. "There is no difference between love and joy" (T-5.In.2:3).

Love also contains peace. Because love fulfills all need, it allows the mind to rest and be at peace. Also, to love something is to be at peace with what it is. And because of this peace with it, we do not attack it, do not make war on it.

Heaven, then, being love, is also peace. It is a realm of perfect, undisturbed peace and stillness, in which no disruption or difference can enter.

> The still infinity of endless peace surrounds you gently in its soft embrace, so strong and quiet, tranquil in the might of its Creator, nothing can intrude upon the sacred Son of God within. (T-29.V.2:4)
>
> Heaven is perfectly unambiguous. Everything is clear and bright, and calls forth one response. There is no darkness and there is no contrast. There is no variation. There is no interruption. There is a sense of peace so deep that no dream in this world has ever brought even a dim imagining of what it is. (T-13.XI.3:8-13)

The Course, in fact, seems to use peace as much or more than love in characterizing Heaven. What is the peace of Heaven like? Mystics and saints throughout history have stated that this "oceanic peace" is indescribable, that it "passeth understanding" (at least intellectual understanding), as Paul said. The Course refers to this fact in the above passage, saying that it is "so deep that no dream in this world has ever brought even a dim imagining of what it is." In another place, the Course makes this point even more clearly:

> God's peace is recognized at first by just one thing; in every way it is totally unlike all previous experiences. It calls to mind nothing that went before. It brings with it no past associations. It is a new thing entirely. (M-20.2:2-5)

Yet, though inscrutable, the Course says there is a way to gain "the faintest intimation" of what this peace is like:

> Can you imagine what a state of mind without illusions is? How it would feel? Try to remember when there was a time,—perhaps a minute, maybe even less—when nothing came to interrupt your peace; when you were certain you were loved and safe. Then try to picture what it would be like to have that moment be extended to the end of time and to eternity. Then let the sense of quiet that you felt be multiplied a hundred times, and then be multiplied another hundred more.
>
> And now you have a hint, not more than just the faintest intimation of the state your mind will rest in when the truth has come. (W-pI.107.2:1-3:1)

This passage serves to answer the common complaint that Heaven sounds boring. When you hear that there is no form and no change, it sounds like Heaven is comparable to watching snow on your TV set for about a million years. For the forms and the action on the set are what interest us. Yet Heaven is not the absence of positive experience. It is *unlimited* positive experience. It is formless and changeless because form and change are types of limitation. Heaven, as the above passage implies, is like taking your most peaceful moment and expanding it to become a constant state, and multiplying it to the point where all limitation drops away, so that your peace becomes infinite as well as eternal—formless and changeless.

It is no wonder the Course tells us that we are presently unable to fathom the experience of Heaven, and that, if we could, we would "rush to meet" it without hesitancy or reservation:

> O my brothers, if you only knew the peace that will envelop you and hold you safe and pure and lovely in the Mind of God, you could but rush to meet Him where His altar is. (C-4.8:1)

> O my child, if you knew what God wills for you, your joy would be complete!...Your heart will be so filled with joy that it will leap into Heaven, and into the Presence of God. I cannot tell you what this will be like, for your heart is not ready. (T-11.III.3:1, 5-6)

Summary

Thus, the Course's picture of reality is one of a timeless, spaceless realm, in which no differentiation is possible. More commonly, however, the Course talks about it as Heaven, the Kingdom of God. God is the Lord of Heaven, the Author of reality, Who in a timeless process perpetually extends His Love ever outward, giving birth to "new" creation. We can almost picture concentric waves of Divine Love radiating out, first in the creation of the Son, and then in the Son's creations, so that this Love continues to roll outward forever, past all limits, "beyond infinity, where time and distance have no meaning" (S-3.IV.8:2).

In the Kingdom of God, oneness reigns. There are creations, but they remain connected to God, inside of God, one with God, made of God. They are His children, who look on Him with awe; yet they are His equals, for in creating them He gave all of Himself away. There are parts, but each part is one with all other parts, and each one is somehow simultaneously the whole. Any kind of partiality or distinction is lost as each thing extends "outward" in all directions in a timeless sharing of love. We, the parts, are forever giving all of ourselves away to the totality of the All. We are thus part of the pure givingness of Heaven, of Love's uniting with Itself. And as we give what we have received, Love's abundance overflows, Its fullness increases, and God's Kingdom expands outward.

Yet paradoxically, this extension and increase are taking place *within* God. For His infinitely numbered Sons and the Sons of His Sons are all merely parts of Him. And so, even after all of this creation, extension, and expansion, there is still only the One. There is only God. "Beyond the First there is no other, for there is no order, no second or third, and nothing but the First" (T-14.IV.1:8).

Chapter 4
The Criteria for What Is Real

The Course is not just saying that Heaven is real. It is saying that Heaven is the *only* reality. And, in my eyes, it is going a step farther. It is suggesting that Heaven is the only thing that *could possibly* be real, that is, according to the Course's standards. What are these standards? From what I can see, the Course has adopted two uncompromising, almost ruthless, criteria by which to measure whether or not something qualifies as real. If something meets those criteria, it is real. If not, it is pure illusion. Let us take a look at these two criteria.

I. Only What God Creates Is Real

This first criterion was more or less stated in the last chapter. God is the Author of reality, the Prime Creator (T-7.I.7:6). He is not constrained by any outside laws, rules, precedents, or dissenting voices. He is absolutely free to create as He pleases. Whatever He says, goes. His Thought instantaneously becomes permanent, eternal reality. And if something is not His Thought, it simply is not real: "What is real except the creations of God?" (T-8.VI.5:6). As we saw, God creates only like Himself, only the infinite, the eternal, and the perfect. Therefore, nothing else can be real.

We can think of this first criterion as, in a sense, a religious one. It is based on faith in God's ultimate power. Only here, that faith is taken to a nontraditional extreme, an extreme which is really a testimony to the awe which the Course reserves for God. Normally we think that all kinds of beings have power to change reality. Since we believe that this world is real, and since every living thing can exert an effect on this world, we believe that everything that creeps, crawls, swims, and flies has the power to shape reality itself. A dung beetle that has rolled a little ball of dung from one spot to another has therefore exercised creative power! The Course, however, says that only God—along with His extensions working in unison with Him—has this power. Only God can produce real effects.

II. What Is Real Must Be Perfectly Consistent and Coherent

This second criterion—which I will spend the rest of the chapter on—is philosophical, rather than religious. It makes an appeal to our own faculty of reason. As such, our discussion of it is going to be unusually intellectual and abstract. Yet I hope that if you pay careful attention, it will be rewarding.

Throughout the Course there are literally hundreds of passages that, if read sensitively, imply that only transcendental reality makes any sense at all. And we do not mean Divine, transcendental sense; we mean *normal, everyday sense*. To find an example we need go no farther than the Introduction to the Text. There we are told:

> *Nothing real can be threatened.*
> *Nothing unreal exists.* (T-In.2:2-3)

The more one looks at these sentences, the more one can see that they are intended to be statements of pure and obvious logic. This is obviously so with the second sentence, but is also true of the first. Think about the word "threatened." To threaten something is to face it with destruction, with becoming nonexistent or unreal. Thus, in saying that nothing real can be threatened, the Course is making a simple statement that nothing *real* can be faced with becoming *unreal*. We therefore can rephrase those sentences in this way:

> *What is real cannot be unreal.*
> *What is unreal is unreal.*

How simple. The implication in this passage, and scores of others, is that if we just brushed up on our logic and reason, our minds, in a blaze of insight, would realize that anything but Heaven is logically absurd. In other words, pure logic can establish the sole existence of transcendental reality. What a radical claim! If true, this would mean that to believe in the Course's view of reality one need not swallow any faith assumptions. One need only be open to hard, objective logic (although the Course has nothing against faith assumptions).

Certainly this is an odd combination—the combination of logic, reason, and proof with a realm that is beyond all intellectual concepts and distinctions. Yet this is also quite characteristic of the Course, which itself uses rigorous logic (even formal syllogisms), and tells us that the Holy Spirit also uses "impeccable" logic (T-5.V.1:4). The Course further claims that true reason is something we are currently incapable of, being an ability that "lies in the other self you have cut off from your awareness" (T-21.V.4:2). It even says that "God does not contradict Himself" (T-8.VI.7:5), but instead thinks with "perfect consistency" (T-7.II.7:1).

Many years ago when I first sensed that such a proof was in the Course, my mind was tantalized. Much of my background is in philosophy, and the idea that there could be a proof for transcendental reality captivated me. I had always resonated with Descartes and his attempt to build a whole system out of a single fact that could not be doubted: "I think, therefore I am." Now I began to see that the author of the Course also resonated with such an attempt. He even spoke approvingly of Descartes' method to Helen and Bill (see *Absence from Felicity*, p. 267), and paraphrased Descartes' central insight in the Course itself: "If I did not think I would not exist, because life is thought" (W-pI.54.2:3). And yet, my sense was that with the Course's author, we are dealing with a mind of immeasurably greater power and insight. I felt therefore that if I could just grasp what he was saying, I would be glimpsing a great philosophical truth.

It has taken me many years of detective work, however, to figure out what the Course really is saying in this case. In the end, it proved so simple yet so radical that my mind had great difficulty grasping it. Only by collecting an ever-growing number of relevant passages, and then identifying certain passages that were essentially spoon-feeding me the answer, was I able to solve the puzzle.

The Principles of Sense or Meaning

As a background for understanding this second criterion, let us examine how we normally judge the truth or falsity of statements.

There are some very simple rules we use to decide whether or not a statement is true. Before we even bother to check a statement against sensory "reality," we evaluate the statement's internal structure; we see whether or not it makes sense, whether or not it has any meaning. There are two kinds of sense or meaning that I want to point out.

The first is *internal consistency*. This means that a statement does not contradict itself. If the same statement says two incompatible things, then we figure that statement cannot possibly be true. Imagine someone telling you, "My car is across town sitting in the shop right now, and that is why I just drove it over here to your house." The two parts of the statement contradict each other. They cannot both be true. Yet the statement claims that they are both true. And so the statement itself must be false.

Some other examples: "Since all men are mortal, and Socrates is a man, Socrates must be immortal." "My hamster physically died yesterday, but his heart, lungs, brain, and muscles never stopped functioning" (that would make a great story for the tabloids). "I went to the store and purchased apples for a dollar apiece. I gave them a dollar and got ten apples." If the words in these statements are taken in their normal sense, the statements cannot be true, for by asserting two things that cannot go together, they are really saying nothing. Contradictory statements are nonsense, non-statements.

The Course highly values the principle of non-contradiction, using the word "contradict" and its variants over eighty times, and saying that "Understanding means consistency because God means consistency" (T-7.V.6:11); and "God made no contradictions" (W-pI.131.7:2). It, in fact, contains many references to the fact that a contradictory statement is meaningless. For instance:

> An "unwilling will" does not mean anything, being a contradiction in terms that actually means nothing. (T-8.VI.7:1)

> The "fearful healer" is a contradiction in terms [since healing is release from fear], and is therefore a concept that only a conflicted mind could possibly perceive as meaningful. (T-7.V.5:10)

The other kind of sense is *coherence* or cohesion, as opposed to chaotic, meaningless nonsense. Incoherence is where parts of a statement do not so much contradict each other, as they simply do not meaningfully relate to each other. For example (to randomly pick from my dictionary), "Orchestration Faustian godfather jujitsu dogmatize." In that sentence, the words simply do not relate to each other. They do not form a meaningful or coherent whole. When you encounter such a statement, you automatically assume it cannot be true, because it is not really saying anything at all. There is nothing there to *be* true.

The Course also places immense value on coherence, on aspects of a whole being in meaningful relationship. There are a great many passages in the Course that reflect this value. Here are a couple:

> The ego attacks everything it perceives by breaking it into small, disconnected parts, without meaningful relationships and therefore without meaning. The ego will always substitute chaos for meaning. (T-11.V.13:5-6)

> This is characteristic of the ego's judgments. Separately, they seem to hold, but put them together and the system of thought that arises from joining them is incoherent and utterly chaotic. For form is not enough for meaning, and the underlying lack of content makes a cohesive system impossible. (T-14.X.9:1-3)

Both consistency and coherence are closely related. Both say, quite simply, that the parts of a statement have to fit together if the statement is to make sense. Contradiction and incoherence are simply two different ways in which parts do not go together, in which the whole does not make sense. Consistency and coherence are merely two ways in which parts go together, producing a whole that is meaningful. And in the end these two ways are distinct from each other. Where contradiction ends and incoherence begins is often impossible to tell. They blend into each other.

My point about these two kinds of sense is that they are essentially laws of mind. Everyone uses them all the time. Whether or not you are consciously aware of it, you are continually using them to evaluate statements, even the statements I am making now. In fact, you cannot *not* use them. Even if you were to verbally deny the validity of these laws, you would probably support your denial with a statement that was designed to be internally consistent and coherent! You certainly would not say, "Orchestration Faustian godfather jujitsu dogmatize."

Because they are laws of mind, when statements violate these laws it is really impossible for our minds to consider those statements to be true. Think of the examples I have used above. Unless you twist the words around to mean something other than what is intended, your mind simply cannot accept those statements as true. That is because, as I said earlier, they are not really statements. By not saying anything consistent or coherent, they do not say anything at all. They are simply nonsense parading as meaningful statements. The point here, to speak it very plainly, is that *nonsensical statements about reality cannot be true*.

What, then, if we were to take these rules of thinking to their logical extreme? What if we were to apply them with far greater rigor and consistency than we normally would dream of doing? Would they tell us anything about the nature of reality?

This is precisely what the Course does. It takes the most basic and unavoidable rules of thinking and simply carries them out more sweepingly and uncompromisingly than we would normally consider doing. And the results are earthshaking. We will look at these results first under the heading of consistency and then under the heading of coherence.

Consistency

Reality must be consistent. It cannot contradict itself. We assume this with every thought we think and every sentence we utter. This, in fact, is a guiding assumption behind modern science. It is the reason that science can successfully use mathematics to describe the physical world. Yet I think the Course would say that we do not normally fathom the full implications of this fact. We do not normally apply the rule of consistency as perfectly as we could. We are quite prone to making exceptions, and exceptions are inconsistencies, contradictions. To make any sense, the rule of consistency must be applied *consistently*.

What would it look like to allow no contradictions whatsoever? To begin with, we would have to get rid of opposites. We would have to disallow the idea that two opposing qualities or attributes can both exist. Normally, we are amazingly lax about this. Love and hate, good and evil, life and death, mind and matter—these are the stuff of reality as we see it. We are quite comfortable with the idea that such opposites can exist side by side. Yet that is a contradiction. Only one side of any of those pairs can be true. As the Course says in talking about life and death:

> For death is total. Either all things die, or else they live and cannot die. No compromise is possible. For here again we see an obvious position, which we must accept if we be sane; what contradicts one thought entirely can not be true, unless its opposite is proven false.
> (W-pI.163.6:2-5)

Let us look at the implications of this line of thought. The following passage is an excellent introduction, being perhaps the most important and revealing passage on this subject:

> Power cannot oppose. For opposition would weaken it, and weakened power is a contradiction in ideas. Weak strength is meaningless....Power is unopposed, to be itself. No weakness can intrude on it without changing it into something it is not. To weaken is to limit, and impose an opposite that contradicts the concept that it attacks. And by this does it join to the idea a something it is not, and make it unintelligible. Who can understand a double concept, such as "weakened power" or "hateful love?"
>
> You have decided that your brother is a symbol for a "hateful-love," a "weakened-power," and above all, a "living-death." And so he has no meaning to you, for he stands for what is meaningless. He represents a double thought, where half is canceled out by the remaining half. Yet even this is quickly contradicted by the half it canceled out, and so they both are gone. And now he stands for nothing. Symbols which but represent ideas that cannot be must stand for empty space and nothingness. (T-27.III.1:1-2:6)

I never cease to be amazed by this passage. In one sweep, it shows us the real power of the Course's thought. Do you see the implications that are opened up by consistently applying the rule of consistency? Do you see the implications for the nature of reality?

Opposites involve us in a contradiction. That much is plain. In the case of the above example, combining the attribute of power with the attribute of weakness is a logical contradiction. They cannot both be true.

The direct result of this is that any real attribute or thing must be *total*. It cannot be partial or halfway. For then it has been mixed with an opposite, and that is a logical contradiction. For instance, the idea of power itself does not contain the idea of weakness. Power is just power. And so the only way you can get power that is only halfway powerful is if you put weakness together with power, if you dilute power with weakness. Yet a "weakened-power" is meaningless. It is a contradiction, "a double thought, where half is canceled out by the remaining half" which "is quickly contradicted by the half it canceled out." Thus, what is real must be total.

> I have stated that the basic concepts referred to in this course are not matters of degree. Certain fundamental concepts cannot be understood in terms of opposites. It is impossible to conceive of light and darkness or everything and nothing as joint possibilities [for they contradict each other]. They are all true or all false.
>
> Innocence is not a partial attribute. It is not real *until* it is total. (T-3.II.1:1-4, 2:1-2)

"Total," in my mind, implies two things. First, it implies that something is *undiluted* or pure. Second, it implies that something is *unlimited* or infinite. Any thing or attribute in reality would have to be absolutely pure and completely unlimited, or else it would be diluted and limited by its opposite.

Let us then imagine two lists of the possible attributes of reality. On one list would be love, life, light, holiness, peace, joy, power, knowledge. On the other list would be their opposites: hate, death, darkness, sin, war, depression, weakness, and uncertainty. If we are to allow no contradictions, and hence no opposites, only one of these lists can be true. Which one? This is not difficult to decide, for, as the Course says more than once, it is literally impossible to make the things on the second list total:

> If fear and love cannot coexist, and if it is impossible to be wholly fearful and remain alive, the only possible whole state is that of love. (T-5.In.2:2)

> It is impossible to conceive of light and darkness or everything and nothing as joint possibilities. They are all true or all false. It is essential that you realize your thinking will be erratic until a firm commitment to one or the other is made. A firm commitment to darkness or nothingness, however, is impossible. No one has ever lived who has not experienced *some* light or *some* thing. No one, therefore, is able to deny truth totally, even if he thinks he can. (T-3.II.1:3-8)

Another way of making the same point is to say that weakness, depression, etc., are inconceivable without their opposites—without power and joy—being a denial of those opposites, the absence of them. For instance, implicit in all depression is the desire for joy. Therefore, you cannot have total weakness and total depression. Yet joy can be total. It (at least in principle) can be free of the fear of, or desire for, depression. Thus, if only the first list of attributes can be total, and if reality must be total, then only the first list can be real.

Reality, then, has to be love, life, light, holiness, peace, joy, power, knowledge. And all of these attributes must be total, which means undiluted and unlimited. Further, these attributes cannot in any way contradict or oppose each other. They must be perfectly compatible with each other; so compatible, in fact, that they are perfectly united. Or else there would be some small bit of contradiction, which would result in nonsense and unreality.

In fact, perfect consistency—total lack of contradiction—would allow for no real differences in reality whatsoever. For any real difference would be an opposition, a contradiction. Thus all the myriad forms of difference that exist in this world cannot exist in reality. As the Course states, reality can have no "degrees, aspects and intervals" (T-3.IV.1:5), "no kinds nor levels, no divergencies and no distinctions. It is like itself, unchanged throughout" (W-pI.127.1:4-5). One kind of difference that the Course especially targets is the idea of levels or orders of reality, saying that those orders would necessarily contradict each other.

> Spirit has no levels, and all conflict arises from the concept of levels. Only the Levels of the Trinity are capable of unity. The levels created by the separation

> cannot but conflict [or contradict]. This is because they are meaningless to each other. (T-3.IV.1:6-9)

> Opposing [or contradicting] orders of reality make reality meaningless, and reality *is* meaning. (T-9.I.13:6)

Therefore, for reality to be completely consistent, it must contain nothing but pure, flawless, unbroken, seamless *consistency*, absolute sameness; in short, *perfect oneness*, "the perfect consistency of the Kingdom" (T-7.II.7:1).

Another result of accepting no contradictions would be to get rid of the idea of change. Let's face it, change is the ultimate contradiction. Under careful analysis, change makes no sense. It is a meaningless idea. When something changes, what it was passes away. What was real has become unreal. Further, its new self emerges out of nowhere, out of unreality. What was unreal is now real. Does any of this really make sense? Nothing turning into something, something coming out of nothing. The real being unreal and unreal being real. It is all a crazy contradiction. It is this nonsensical nature of change, and hence of time itself, that the Course is talking about in the following passages: "Time is a trick, a sleight of hand, a vast illusion in which figures come and go as if by magic" (W-pI.158.4:1). "For everything you see will change, and yet you thought it real before, and now you think it real again" (T-30.VIII.1:4).

Change is inconstancy, inconsistency. It is thus *contradiction*. Change is contradiction over time. As a result, changelessness is one of the Course's basic and recurring criteria for what is real, as we see in the following passage:

> [Reality] cannot change with time or mood or chance. Its changelessness is what makes it real. This cannot be undone. Undoing is for unreality. (T-14.IX.2:7-10)

This explains why nothing real can be threatened. For the idea of the real being threatened with becoming unreal is a contradiction. The real cannot be unreal. And so the real cannot change.

In summary, since contradiction is impossible, reality must be "one, without an opposite" (T-26.III.1:8). Reality must be pure, total, maximal love, peace, power, knowledge, and holiness—undiluted and unlimited. And it must be changeless, for change is contradiction over time. And this can have no exceptions, for exceptions are contradictions. "Truth must be all-inclusive, if it be the truth at all. Accept no opposites and no exceptions, for to do so is to contradict the truth entirely" (W-pI.152.2:6-7).

Coherence

Let us now apply the idea of coherence or cohesion with the same uncompromising rigor. As a start, let us look more closely at what makes for coherence. A whole is coherent when its parts are in a meaningful relationship with each other. Parts make up a whole, and wherever parts join or touch, they must be in a meaningful relationship. And this means that they must have a related meaning, a shared meaning. This is what allows for the whole to be coherent, integrated, organized, *whole*.

For example, look at the sentence, "The wheel spun on the axle." "Wheel" and "spun" are parts that meaningfully relate, because wheels are things that do, in fact, spin. "Spin" is part of the meaning of "wheel." "Spun on" and "axle" also are parts that meaningfully relate, because axles are things that other things spin on. The same with "the wheel" and "on the axle," because wheels do go on axles. In all cases, then, the parts that are placed together actually go together, because they have related meanings, a shared meaning.

However, if you were to stick a part in that did not have a related meaning, you would get incoherence, nonsense. For example (to randomly pick from my dictionary again), "The wheel spun on the oncology." That does not make a lot of sense. Or, "The wheel spun on the rhesus monkey." Now, that does not make much sense, but you can imagine it making some sense. Even though spinning wheels do not go too well with rhesus monkeys, it is possible to imagine a wheel spinning on one.

This gives us a clue about the nature of meaning. The more the parts meaningfully relate, the more meaning is produced. The more of a shared or related meaning they have, the more sense they make. If the parts have only a partly shared meaning, they produce only a partly meaningful whole.

Now all of us would admit that the world contains a great deal of chaos and nonsense. However, in light of what we have just seen, even the most organized wholes of this world contain only partial meaning. And partial meaning means part coherence and part incoherence. For instance, as we saw, the wheel of a car has a shared meaning with the axle of a car. But it has less of a shared meaning with the car's ash tray. There is thus incoherence in the wheel/ash tray relationship. And even the shared meaning of wheel and axle is only partial. Their meanings are not totally shared, totally overlapping. For they are different things, with different meanings that only somewhat overlap. Because of this it is possible, and quite easy, for them to separate from each other. If their relationship was total—if their meanings, their identities, were totally related—how could they ever separate? Parts that can disassemble and reassemble in different configurations cannot be totally meaningfully related, just as people who divorce could not have been perfectly married. Perfect coherence would make separation impossible. If any whole in this world contained pure, absolute coherence, how could it ever become incoherent—how could its parts ever fall apart? By these standards, nothing in this world, especially not my car, is fully coherent.

Partially related parts produce partly incoherent wholes. And how can a whole be truly coherent if its makeup is even partly incoherent? To refer back to our discussion of consistency, wholes that are both meaningful *and* meaningless are a contradiction. They are thus meaningless, and hence unreal.

All wholes in our world, then, are incoherent. In talking about the chaotic nature of this world, the Course especially likes to target our thoughts, since it claims that our thoughts made this world. It says, "They blow across his mind like wind-swept leaves that form a patterning an instant, break apart to group again, and scamper off" (W-pI.186.9:5); "They fuse and merge and separate, in shifting and totally meaningless patterns that need not be judged at all" (T-18.I.7:7). In light of the chaotic nature of our thinking, here is how the Course characterizes our making of the world:

> He does not realize he picked a thread from here, a scrap from there, and wove a picture out of nothing. For the parts do not belong together, and the whole contributes nothing to the parts to give them meaning. (T-24.V.2:3-4)

What would absolute coherence—coherence carried to its logical extreme—look like? Each part would have to be so meaningfully related to every other part, that their meaning would be *totally* shared. Thus, parts would have to be *equal* to each other, *identical* to each other and *joined* with each other. Each part would so totally meaningfully relate to every other part, that each part would simultaneously be the whole. Now *that* would be coherence.

Absolute coherence, then, just like absolute consistency, would be the same as perfect, flawless, unbroken *oneness*. It would correspond exactly to the perfect unity of Heaven which we discussed in the last chapter.

The Course's main focus in relation to coherence, however, is not on the whole, but on the parts. Its main point, referred to scores and scores of times in several different forms, is that a part that is disconnected from the meaning of the whole is meaningless. Just as a whole with unrelated parts is nonsensical, so the reverse is true: parts not integrated into a whole are meaningless, and must therefore be illusory.

To state this more fully, meaning lies in wholeness. Since meaning only comes from parts joining together, parts *by themselves* cannot be truly meaningful. They only become meaningful by their participation in the whole. By having a place in the whole they are able to partake in the meaning of the whole, able to share in its meaning. As the Course says, a part needs "the whole to give it any meaning, for by itself it does mean nothing" (T-18.VIII.5:3). As was implied in a passage quoted above, parts have no meaning unless "the whole contributes...to the parts to give them meaning" (T-24.V.2:4).

Going back to our wheel example, does a wheel have meaning by itself? Think about a wheel completely by itself, not being part of anything else, not affecting anything whatsoever, having no function in a larger whole. It is meaningless. A wheel only has meaning as it spins on an axle so that it can help a car move along the road, so that the car can get someone to a destination, so that he can perform a certain task and thereby achieve a certain goal, so that this goal can contribute to his life and the lives of others, etc., etc. The wheel only has meaning as it takes its part in a larger whole.

For this reason, separate parts can have no meaning. A separate part is "a distorted fragment of the whole without the meaning that the whole would give" (T-22.III.4:3). It is "separate and therefore without meaning" (T-11.II.3:2). "Small disconnected parts [are] without meaningful relationships and therefore without meaning"

(T-11.V.13:5). And if separate parts have no meaning, then *separate parts cannot be real.* Anything that exists in isolation cannot be real.

This is why, as the Course says over and over, only what is shared is real: "Except you share it, nothing can exist" (T-28.V.1:10); "It is not shared, and so it is not real" (T-13.X.2:10). This is also why, as the Course also repeatedly states, only what causes effects beyond itself can be real, for what affects nothing else must be *in relationship* with nothing else.

> What has no effects does not exist. Laws do not operate in a vacuum, and what leads to nothing has not happened. If reality is recognized by its extension, what leads to nothing could not be real. (T-11.V.2:5-7)

This also explains the idea (mentioned in the last chapter, and referred to in the above passage) that only what extends can be real. For it is through extending outward into the whole that a part transcends isolation, separateness, part-ness, and truly participates in the whole and its meaningfulness.

Since separate parts do not make sense, reality can have no separate parts. "It is *not* made up of different parts" (T-18.VI.8:6). "It is all one and has no separate parts" (T-3.V.8:7). And yet, the condition of this world is one of separate parts. Everything is a separate part, somewhat connected to other parts, but still distinct and relatively independent.

> Each tiny fragment seems to be self-contained, needing another for some things, but by no means totally dependent on its one Creator for everything; needing the whole to give it any meaning, for by itself it does mean nothing. Nor has it any life apart and by itself. (T-18.VIII.5:3-4)

According to this argument, then, a world made up of separate parts does not make sense and simply cannot be real. And we cannot be separate individuals, dangling free and independent of the whole.

Commentary on the Second Criterion

I find this second criterion for what is real to be most profound. The greatest rational arguments begin with the familiar, and through simple, elegant means bring you irresistibly to the radical and unfamiliar. And this is exactly what this argument does. It begins with the most simple, the most basic, the most familiar rules of thinking, rules we use in thinking every thought and constructing every sentence. And then by simply applying these rules uncompromisingly, without exception, it draws us to a radical yet irresistible conclusion.

That conclusion is basically two-fold. First, only a realm of seamless consistency and absolute coherence or wholeness can be real. The main quality of this realm is that it contains no differences, for differences produce contradictions and incoherence. As the Course says, "Illusions are always illusions of differences. How could it be otherwise?" (M-8.2:1-2). Thus, as we saw, there can be no opposites, no partiality, no limits, no degrees, no levels, no change, no chaos, and no separate parts. Only perfect sameness, wholeness, oneness, can be real.

The second part of the conclusion is that this world is quite simply senseless, meaningless. For it is made of nothing but differences:

> The basis for the world's perception...rests on differences; on uneven background and shifting foreground, on unequal heights and diverse sizes, on varying degrees of darkness and light, and thousands of contrasts in which each thing seen competes with every other in order to be recognized. A larger object overshadows a smaller one. A brighter thing draws the attention from another with less intensity of appeal....What the body's eyes behold is only conflict. Look not to them for peace and understanding. (M-8.1)

This is a world full of opposites and contradictions, "a battleground, where contradictions reign and opposites make endless war" (M-27.2:7). It is a world of shades of gray, where everything is partial, ambivalent, ambiguous. It is a world awash in ceaseless change, "in which figures come and go as if by magic" (W-pI.158.4:1), magically appearing out of nothing and then magically passing back into nothing. It is full of incoherence: even its most organized wholes must eventually fall apart under the weight of their own chaos. It is made up of separate, disconnected parts, floating free, "without the meaning that the whole would give" (T-22.III.4:3). The Course summarizes it well: "The world you made is therefore totally chaotic, governed by arbitrary and senseless 'laws,' and without meaning of any kind" (T-12.III.9:6).

In short, as we have probably been saying all our lives, this world is crazy, it makes no sense. "Reason would tell you that the world you see...must make no sense to you" (T-22.I.2:3). This can give us a much greater appreciation of what the Course means when it says that this world is insane. The world is not only insane in that it violates the nature of transcendental reality; it even violates the most fundamental rules of the human mind. "What makes no sense and has no meaning is insanity" (T-25.VII.3:5). This world is made of the stuff of madness.

Yet, being senseless, it cannot be real. "And what is madness cannot be the truth" (T-25.VII.3:6). Just as we cannot imagine a meaningless sentence being real, *so we must admit that a meaningless world cannot be real.* To assert that this world is real is like boldly proclaiming, "Orchestration Faustian godfather jujitsu dogmatize," and thinking that you had made a meaningful statement about the nature of reality. As the Course says, "a meaningless world is impossible. Nothing without meaning exists" (W-pI.13.1:2-3). "That is all the world of the ego is. Nothing. It has no meaning. It does not exist" (T-7.VI.11:4-7).

As we will see in Part II, as citizens of this world, we are literally running around inside a meaningless sentence, a nonsensical mental construction. As we walk through the world, we are walking through a jumble of our own insane thoughts. Shakespeare was right. Life in this world "is a tale told by an idiot, full of sound and fury, signifying nothing." And we are the idiot.

Transcendental reality is real and only that can be real. This is certainly a radical conclusion to any logical argument. Yet in the simplicity and elegance of this argument, as well as in its absolutely uncompromising nature and its radical, sweeping conclusion, we have a window onto the mind of the Course's author. That author, Jesus, must be in a state of the purest consistency, without any exceptions, any contradictions, any disturbance in the pure light of consistency. He must be in a state of absolute wholeness, in which no parts dangle meaninglessly outside of the whole, in which chaos is unthinkable; a state in which one step outside of this perfect oneness is instantly recognized as a descent into pure nonsense.

This, I believe, is where the Course's all-or-nothing character comes from. It is so absolute and so uncompromising simply because its author refuses to descend into any sort of nonsense. And in his complete refusal to tolerate exceptions, inconsistencies and nonsense, he asks us to do the same:

> You may believe that this position is extreme, and too inclusive to be true. Yet can truth have exceptions?...Truth must be all-inclusive, if it be the truth at all. Accept no opposites and no exceptions, for to do so is to contradict the truth entirely.
>
> Salvation is the recognition that the truth is true, and nothing else is true. This you have heard before, but may not yet accept both parts of it. Without the first, the second has no meaning. But without the second, is the first no longer true. Truth cannot have an opposite. This can not be too often said and thought about. For if what is not true is true as well as what is true, then part of truth is false. And truth has lost its meaning. Nothing but the truth is true, and what is false is false. (W-pI.152.2-3)

Jesus then adds that this simple distinction appears obscure only because of our own hidden choices. These make truth appear "to have some aspects that belie consistency, but do not seem to be but contradictions introduced by you" (W-pI.152.4:4).

All of this greatly helps to clarify the relationship between the intellect and Heaven. It is a frequent assumption these days that since Heaven transcends the intellect, the intellect must be the very antithesis of Heaven. It is the Anti-Christ, to be laid aside as soon as one decides to stop playing around and really seek God. Yet this second criterion reveals that the Course's attitude is really quite different. For here we see a continuum between earthly thinking and heavenly knowledge, in which Heaven's laws are actually the same as the most basic rules of intellectual thinking. Heaven just follows them better! In trying to think accurately, then, we are groping to obey the laws of heavenly knowledge. And if thinking were carried out with perfect consistency, all distinctions would disappear, subject and object would unite, and the intellect would be transcended. That is how Heaven transcends the intellect, not by negating it, but by exceeding it at its own game.

Personally, I find this criterion for what is real to be extremely inspiring. Being intellectually oriented, I have always found our world depressing. For this world just presents us with too many things for the mind to stumble over, too many things to regret, to recoil from, to have to make excuses for. It is a "reality" that must forever disappoint, for it simply does not live up to the mind's highest sensibilities. Innate in the mind is the yearning for the ultimate, for the flawless, for that which has no inconsistencies and no lacks. The mind, by its very nature, yearns for the perfect. Now, in light of this criterion in the Course, I see that not only is the perfect real, but, according to the laws of mind, only the perfect *can* be real. What a wonderful, beautiful idea: Only the unopposed, the total, the pure, the infinite, the maximal, the changeless, the complete—*the perfect; only that can be real.*

Chapter 5
The Goal of Goals

So far we have seen several ideas that characterize reality in the Course's view: oneness, love, extension; that what is real is created by God and is like God; that what is real is consistent and coherent. As a final reflection on the nature of reality, it has occurred to me that all of these ideas have a shared meaning. This shared meaning is surprisingly simple: *everything in reality goes together*. It all fits, it is all compatible.

The idea of oneness obviously echoes this, for things that are one are things that go together completely. The same with love: when you love something you are perceiving a fit between you and it that makes you want to be together with it. And so you extend outward to it, to bring the two of you together. "For it is the function of love to unite all things unto itself, and to hold all things together" (T-12.VIII.7:11).

Even our criteria from the last chapter fit into this model. Our first criterion is that what is real is what proceeds from God and is like God. To restate this: only what fits with God, only what goes together with God, is real. Our second criterion was consistency and coherence. And both of these, as we said, are merely ways in which parts fit, in which they go together.

Oddly enough, then, the mystic's notion of pure oneness, the heart's ideal of pure love, the will's dynamic of extension, the religious criterion of God's absolute power, and the intellect's measure of consistency and coherence, *all yield the exact same reality*: reality is a domain in which everything fits together.

Yet this obviously puts it much too weakly. For in reality things do not merely go together; they go together *emphatically, ecstatically*. Their fit is all-encompassing, seamless, perfect. It is not just co-existence, it is Embrace. It is not just tolerance, it is Love. The fit is so perfect, the embrace so complete, that any trace of difference, of multiplicity, of two-ness fades away as all things blend into the One.

The Paradox of Unity and Duality

Before Part I concludes I need to admit that the Course's vision of reality is sort of an odd bird. For it combines two very different visions of reality. The first vision one could call a pure nondual vision. As the name "nondual" implies, there is no duality, only oneness. If one were to carry nonduality out to its logical extreme—which I am not sure that any existing traditions really do—one would get only absolute oneness, without the slightest hint of form, change or multiplicity. In this vision, there would be no point in talking about worshipping the Absolute or having a relationship with It, for you are It, period.

The second vision is a dualistic one, in which there is a creator God who creates a multiplicity of children that are distinct from Himself. These children are not God, but they are able to enjoy the nectar of His Presence through being in loving, worshipful relationship with Him.

The Course clearly describes a nondual reality in which there are injected dualistic elements. It clearly describes a Heaven that is pure oneness without any distinctions. Yet it speaks of a God Who creates children that are in some sense distinct from Him and from each other. These children have a relationship with Him, and even stand in worshipful awe of Him.

This leaves the Course's view of reality riddled with paradox. We saw the paradox of sameness and newness in creation, the paradox of equality and inferiority in the Son's relationship with God, the paradox of the many and the one within the Son, and the paradox of parts that are simultaneously the whole. All of these paradoxes are the result of injecting dualistic elements into an essentially nondual vision. And so all of them are a single paradox: the paradox of unity and duality.

The Course, I am sure, would emphatically say that this paradox is not a contradiction. That, in fact, is one definition of what a paradox is: a *seeming* contradiction, one that only *appears* unresolvable. Thus, while contradictions cannot be true, paradoxes can. How, then, can we resolve the paradox of unity and duality? If I may speak for the Course, I would say that somehow Heaven must be able to encompass a trace of dualism and multiplicity *without in the least compromising its fundamental oneness*. This is clearly implied in the following passage, quoted in the last chapter:

> Spirit has no levels, and all conflict arises from the concept of levels. Only the Levels of the Trinity are capable of unity. The levels created by the separation cannot but conflict [or contradict]. (T-3.IV.1:6-8)

In other words, even though levels as we *know them* produce obvious and inevitable contradiction, the Levels of the Trinity do not produce any contradiction whatsoever. We can extend this idea to all of the apparent dualisms we find in the Course's vision of reality.

Is this something we can understand—a nonmultiple multiplicity, a nondual dualism? No, it is obviously beyond our current mental capacity. Yet this need bother us only if we think that our tiny minds are able to wrap themselves around reality. Humility would admit, I think, at least the possibility that reality is bigger than our minds can currently grasp. We can at least entertain the idea that when our minds expand beyond their earthly boundaries, we will see that certain contradictions were just paradoxes, and now make absolute sense.

It is just this humility that the Course is asking of us. For one of its central tenets is the idea that the separated mind has placed itself in a condition of alienation from reality. To awaken, then, we must be willing to recognize that the mind's thoughts, feelings, beliefs, desires, habitual directions, comprehension, and even basic structure, are all fundamentally alienated from reality.

To reiterate what was mentioned in Chapter 2, the reason that our minds cannot currently grasp reality is that they have been placed in a condition of specificity, of part-ness. This part-ness is fundamentally incompatible with reality's condition of totality or all-ness. "The mind that taught itself to think specifically can no longer grasp abstraction in the sense that it is all-encompassing" (W-pI.161.4:7).

Thus, even though the Course gives us a great many conceptual models for understanding reality, we must constantly realize that they are just models, just fingers pointing at the moon. They are not the moon itself. It is easy to forget this, since the Course talks so much about the Father and the Son, about creation and extension, Heaven and eternity. It says so much about Heaven that one can forget that all of those words are merely fingers meant to point the mind up into the sky, far beyond where its current comprehension can go.

The Experience of Heaven

Thus, words about Heaven are not the experience of Heaven. And, as the Course says, "It is this experience toward which the Course is directed. Here alone consistency becomes possible because here alone uncertainty ends" (C-Intro.2:6-7).

It is the experience of reality that we are really seeking, not concepts about reality. In urging us to pursue this experience, the Course is at one with the mystics of the world. Like the mystics, the Course tells us that along the path we can expect to have brief glimpses of the heavenly state, and that these will become increasingly frequent as our minds become more and more transparent to reality: "As this experience increases [in frequency]...all goals but this become of little worth" (W-pI.157.7:1).

This is commonly called the mystical experience. The Course calls it revelation, meaning not God's revealing of inspired words and ideas (as "revelation" traditionally denotes), but God's direct and total revelation of Himself, of His Heart to our hearts. In other words, revelation is the experience of union with God. Like the mystics, the Course has the most hallowed respect for this experience. Lesson 157 in the Workbook ("Into His Presence would I enter now") is dedicated to allowing it to occur. The lesson's introduction reveals the importance placed by the Course on this experience:

> This is a day of silence and of trust. It is a special time of promise in your calendar of days. It is a time Heaven has set apart to shine upon, and cast a timeless light upon this day, when echoes of eternity are heard. This day is holy, for it ushers in a new experience; a different kind of

> feeling and awareness. You have spent long days and nights in celebrating death. Today you learn to feel the joy of life. (W-pI.157.1)

The Course also agrees emphatically with the mystics that the goal of the spiritual path is *continuous* mystical awareness, *permanent* union with God. I believe that the Course parts company with the mystics on the means to that goal. For the Course does not emphasize meditative and contemplative disciplines nearly as much as forgiveness in our relationships. Yet even though there are differences on the means, on the goal there is complete unanimity. Whether we call it Heaven, reality, mystical union, nirvana, samadhi, or some other name, that state of absolute oneness is the goal of spiritual pursuit. It is the state in which existence itself is fulfilled. It is what all living things are searching for in each moment without even knowing it.

Heaven, after all, is our home. Think about that word "home." It implies a world of meaning. Home is where you were born, where you are from. Home is a place designed for you, for your comfort and happiness, where you are surrounded by all that you need and all that interests you. Home is where your family is, those that you belong with, that are like you; those that love and care for you and those that you love in return. Home is shelter, a place of safety where you are protected from all harm. All in all, home is where you belong. It is the place that perfectly fits you, your nature, your needs, your purpose; and that you perfectly fit in return.

The Course is saying that we will never feel truly at home in this world, for it is not our home:

> This world you seem to live in is not home to you. And somewhere in your mind you know that this is true. A memory of home keeps haunting you, as if there were a place that called you to return, although you do not recognize the voice, nor what it is the voice reminds you of. Yet still you feel an alien here, from somewhere all unknown. (W-pI.182.1)

In other words, no matter how much we may think this place is our home, every single person in this world is a homeless person, as the following passage so poignantly describes:

> Here is the only home he thinks he knows. Here is the only safety he believes that he can find. Without the world he made is he an outcast; homeless and afraid. He does not realize that it is here he is afraid indeed, and homeless, too; an outcast wandering so far from home, so long away, he does not realize he has forgotten where he came from, where he goes, and even who he really is.
> (W-pI.166.4)

The Goal of Goals

Given this, the only practical thing to do is to make Heaven our goal. We all know that setting a goal can be very powerful, enabling us to mobilize all of our energies and put them consistently behind one thing. Yet we are accustomed to setting very concrete, short-term goals: for particular relationships, for certain kinds of outer success, for money, cars, houses. These goals, once achieved, leave us wanting more, and so we have to move on to yet another goal.

The Course, in my view, is suggesting that we take the power of goal-setting and put that power behind the Goal of goals, the only goal truly worth achieving: God. Only this goal can satisfy us completely and thus only it can inform and inspire every part of our being, as well as every aspect of our lives. Think of the boldness and courage in setting such a fantastically lofty goal. Just imagine living a life in which each thought, each word and every deed were guided by a single purpose, the goal of transcending our entire phenomenal existence and waking up in Heaven, in the Heart of God. This is precisely what the Course urges us to do:

> *The peace of God is everything I want.*
> *The peace of God is my one goal; the aim*
> *Of all my living here, the end I seek,*
> *My purpose and my function and my life,*
> *While I abide where I am not at home.*
> (W-pI.205.1:2-3)

Pursuit of this goal is immensely facilitated by realizing that, far from being unattainable, it is already accomplished. For, according to the Course, we never physically left Heaven. We are still there, this instant; we are perfect beings this instant. We are in our Father's Arms right now, merely dreaming of being homeless orphans. And it is inevitable that someday we will open our eyes in Heaven and realize that we have been with Him all along. And then we will never sleep again.

The purpose, then, of all these words that I have expended, and that the Course expends, in describing the indescribable, is to help our minds set this goal and devote themselves to it. For if we are going to focus and marshall our energies behind the goal of Heaven, we need something our minds can sink their teeth into, something we can understand—even if it is only a finger, and not the moon. We need reminders of Home, in whatever form they come, be it ideas, poetry, music, images or, best of all, experiential glimpses. And so, hopefully, Part I of this book has served its purpose and stirred within us some distant memory of the forgotten song:

> Listen,—perhaps you catch a hint of an ancient state not quite forgotten; dim, perhaps, and yet not altogether unfamiliar, like a song whose name is long forgotten, and the circumstances in which you heard completely unremembered.
>
> ...Listen, and see if you remember an ancient song you knew so long ago and held more dear than any melody you taught yourself to cherish since.
>
> (T-21.I.6:1, 7:5)

PART II

Chapter 6
The Separation

We saw in Part I that the only thing real, the only thing that *can* be real, is a realm of timeless, formless, changeless, flawless spirit, without any boundaries, lacks, pain, or imperfection.

If this is true, then a whole host of questions should immediately present itself to us: What happened? What are we doing here? How did this world get here? How did it ever come into existence, even *apparent* existence?

Obviously, from the frame of reference of reality, something *lesser* has happened. There has been a kind of descent, or, to put it into more familiar religious terms, a fall. Things started out in a pristine, perfect place and at some point they took a turn for the worse. The Course puts it this way:

> Salvation and forgiveness are the same. They both imply that something has gone wrong; something to be saved from, forgiven for; something amiss that needs corrective change; something apart or different from the Will of God. Thus do both terms imply a thing impossible but yet which has occurred, resulting in a state of conflict seen between what is and what could never be. (W-pI.99.1)

The "something" that went wrong was what the Course calls *the separation*. This was the single event that was responsible for not only our personal condition, but the human condition, the world, and even the entire universe. In ominous words, familiar to most every student of the Course, this event is described:

> Into eternity, where all is one, there crept a tiny, mad idea, at which the Son of God remembered not to laugh. (T-27.VIII.6:2)

The event of the separation is central to the Course and its whole thought system. The Course gives it mythic proportions, referring to it again and again and again, dropping tantalizing hints about it here and there. The Course, in fact, displays almost no interest in history as we know it, except for in history's beginning—the separation—and in its end. For the Course, the separation was the definitive historical event. History was not only set in motion by it; history for the most part is simply one long interminable repetition of it:

> Each day, and every minute in each day, and every instant that each minute holds, you but relive the single instant when the time of terror took the place of love. (T-26.V.13:1)

From what I can see there are two potential explanations for such a full-scale descent from Heaven. One explanation is that it was the result of a Divine plan. In this view, there was some higher reason, conceived by God, for us to journey through the billions of years of the realm of time. The other explanation is that it was something we did strictly on our own; it was our own choice, our own idea, our own initiative.

I personally do not pretend to understand the full and final truth behind the separation. In fact, I will argue later in this book that it simply cannot be understood from within the separated condition. As such, I think there are probably multiple ways to describe it that each have validity, ways that may seem incompatible yet still somehow contain truth.

My task, however, is to represent what the Course has to say about it. And the Course very decidedly uses the second explanation mentioned above. Basically, the Course takes off from the Judaeo-Christian idea of the Fall. Just as Adam and Eve were not following some higher dictate when they ate the apple, so the separation was undertaken by us, apart from God. The idea of the separation, however, is a modification of the idea of the Fall in two important ways.

First, the Course expands and deepens the idea of the Fall. The Course teaches that not only is our inner lack of holiness and harmony with God the result of a fall; but literally *everything* that is not changeless oneness is also. This includes our existence as individual minds inside of biological bodies. Indeed, it includes the very existence and structure of the physical universe of time, space, energy, and matter. It even includes any other nonphysical dimensions or planes, however subtle or rarified, that are not absolutely pure, formless oneness (such as the astral or causal planes of occult lore). In short, everything but perfect oneness is simply an aftereffect, an outpicturing, of the separation.

The second—and more fundamental—way in which the Course modifies the traditional idea of the Fall is that it teaches that the separation was an illusion. It never actually occurred, and so it had no real effects. As a result, we have not really wrecked Heaven, angered God, separated from Him nor corrupted our natures with sin and guilt. The implications of the unreality of the separation are exceedingly deep and far-reaching, and will be a running theme throughout Part II, as well as the principal theme of Chapter 11.

The separation, then, and the universe that resulted from it, had nothing to do with God. Not only does the Course say that God did not create this world, it also never suggests that there was any sort of Divine plan, purpose, or intention behind it. The separation as talked about by the Course was simply the result of a glitch in Heaven, a fly in the celestial ointment. It arose "out of nothingness; an evil flower with no roots at all" (T-24.II.3:3).

In Course terminology, something went awry in the parts of God's Son. The separation, then, was confined to that aspect of Heaven known as the Sonship. And even then, it seems to have had nothing to do with the Christ, the Self of the Sonship. To my knowledge, the Course's consistent implication is that it was strictly the *parts* of the Son—the brothers, the children, the aspects—that caused the separation and produced this world.

In the Beginning

To set the stage for the separation, we have to backtrack a little bit to Part I. To recapitulate, God, in some ineffable, timeless way, extended Himself to create His Son, the Christ. The Son is equal to God, in that God gave His Son all of Himself, and is also less than God, in that God created the Son, the Son did not create God. This Son was single, yet also contained inherent within Him an infinite number of parts. These parts are the crucial thing, since they are the cause of and sole participants in the separation.

The key thing to remember about the parts is their profound and complete connectedness with everything in Heaven. The parts are equal to each other, carbon copies of each other and, in fact, one with each other. Moreover, each part, though in some sense merely a part of the Christ, is also quite literally the whole. And this applies to God also: each part is part of God yet all of God. It receives its being from God, yet in some sense *is* God. Further, each part is in a continual process of extending itself "outward" in an act of joining. This extension is total. Each part gives all of itself away to everything in Heaven all of the time (though, of course, there is no time). The parts extend themselves in a song of love to their fellow parts, to Christ, and to God. And they join with each other and God to give birth through extension to "new" creations, creations which they are equal to, the same as, and one with. Each part is wholly and completely in love with the rest of Heaven. Each part is perfectly consistent with all of reality. Each one is a seamless part of a perfectly coherent whole. And we are the parts.

All of this is a lengthy way to say that we, the parts, are immersed in complete oneness. We are not separate, detachable, or independent, as are parts in this world. We are parts, yet we aren't. If you can just vaguely grasp this single ungraspable idea—of parts that are in some sense distinct yet also completely one—then everything else I have to say about the separation will be understandable, that is, as understandable as it can be.

Specialness

Here, I believe, is how it happened (bear in mind, again, that we are trying to describe the undescribable). We are existing in Heaven in a state of pure oneness. An ocean of God's Love is washing to us, through us, and as us. This Love from our Father gives us our existence, our definition and our joy. This Love is everything to us; it is all there is. Suddenly the thought occurs to us, "I wonder if there could be more than this." We begin to muse further. "Well, God's Love is what makes me happy. Yet I am just one among an infinite number to whom He gives His Love. Perhaps I would be happier if He gave more love to me and less to the others. What if He gave it all just to me? What if I were His favorite son?"

We wanted to be special in Heaven. That was how it all began: with the idea of specialness. "You were at peace until you asked for special favor [from God]" (T-13.III.10:2). The "tiny, mad idea" (T-27.VIII.6:2) that sparked the separation was "the tiny, mad desire to be separate, different and special" (T-25.I.5:5). Thus the universal wish to be special, unique, better than, the wish to have the most likable personality, the sharpest mind, most beautiful body, most prestigious family, most successful job, nicest house, best team, greatest country, etc., etc., is a living fossil, a vestige of the ancient, ancient desire that set this whole thing in motion.

I am sure that this seemed like an innocent desire to minds that had never known anything but perfect oneness. We were searching for something positive, for an increase of our experience of God's Love. My guess is that we had no idea of the consequences, since we had no prior experience with such things as specialness, attack, and guilt. But within the single, seemingly innocuous, request for specialness was contained in seed-form the entire world of pain, fear, and death.

Think about it: the root of the idea of specialness is the idea of specificity, of *separateness*. You cannot be special, unique, superior, unless you are specific, distinct, separate. You cannot be "better than" unless you are "different than." "To 'single out' [the idea of being singled out as God's favorite] is to 'make alone,' and thus make lonely" (T-13.III.12:1).

The idea of specialness, then, was the spark that lit the separation and gave birth to the ego. What is the ego? Simply the belief that we are a separate being, an individual entity, a "limited and separated self" (W-pII.12.1:1). It is the belief that our inner being is completely private, that no one belongs in there but us. It is the conviction that at the root of our nature we are completely alone.

Usurping God's Role as Creator

Of course, God did not grant our request for special favor: "Could He set you apart, knowing that your peace lies in His Oneness? He denied you only your request for pain, for suffering is not of His creation" (T-13.III.12:3-4). God refused to make our specialness real. And so we threw a tantrum. If God will not re-create us as special, we thought, we will just create ourselves. We will reject His stinking Authority. This is why the Course says, "The authority problem is still the only source of conflict" (T-11.In.2:3). And this, the Course says, is the symbology of the story of the Fall in Genesis: "Eating of the fruit of the tree of knowledge is a symbolic expression for usurping the ability for self-creating" (T-3.VII.4:1). According to the Course, our minds went through a series of steps, falling ever deeper into the notion of usurping God's creative power:

> First, you believe that what God created can be changed by your own mind.
>
> Second, you believe that what is perfect can be rendered imperfect or lacking.
>
> Third, you believe that you can distort the creations of God, including yourself.
>
> Fourth, you believe that you can create yourself, and that the direction of your own creation is up to you.
>
> (T-2.I.1:9-12)

This idea of creating ourselves was already implicit in the idea of specialness, for specialness implied a re-creation of our nature. In fact, specialness and usurping God's throne are highly related ideas. And though I am talking as if the less bold and daring idea (specialness) came first, in truth they both imply each other. Specialness seeks to steal status from our fellow parts. Usurpation seeks to steal status from God. Both seek the private, guilty elation of standing victorious at the summit of reality, with our brothers and our Father grovelling at our feet.

Usurpation introduced a new kind of separateness: independence. It said that we were self-sufficient, no longer receiving what we have and what we are from our Creator. The ego, then, was a thought of complete independence, a "terrible autonomy" (W-pII.12.2:4). We were on our own now. We had—in some hard to figure out way—created ourselves, and were unconcerned with the blatant circularity of the idea.

Separateness and Independence

Separateness (from specialness) and independence (from usurpation): these two ideas are both captured in my favorite definition of the ego: "The ego is the mind's belief that it is completely on its own" (T-4.II.8:4). In our eyes we had become tiny separate entities, "self-created, self-sufficient, very vicious and very vulnerable" (T-10.III.4:7). We had become

> self-created, self-maintained, in need of nothing, and unjoined with anything...a separate universe, with all the power to hold itself complete within itself, with every entry shut against intrusion, and every window barred against the light. (T-24.VI.11:2-3)

The ego, then, is basically the idea of being totally on our own, of creating ourselves, defining ourselves, supplying ourselves, and existing by ourselves as our own separate unit. It is a rejection of our inherent oneness with reality, as well as a rejection of our complete dependence on God's creative power. We went from being completely enfolded in boundless oneness to fearfully standing "beyond the Everywhere, apart from All, in separation from the Infinite" (W-pII.12.2:2). In "The Little Garden" section we find a colorful and impactful metaphor for this strange situation:

> This fragment of your mind is such a tiny part of it that, could you but appreciate the whole, you would see instantly that it is like the smallest sunbeam to the sun; or like the faintest ripple on the surface of the ocean. In its amazing arrogance, this tiny sunbeam has decided it is the sun; this almost imperceptible ripple hails itself as the ocean. Think how alone and frightened is this little thought, this infinitesimal illusion, holding itself apart against the universe. The sun becomes the sunbeam's "enemy" that would devour it, and the ocean terrifies the little ripple and wants to swallow it. (T-18.VIII.3:3-6)

Now we can see why it is so important to understand that in Heaven we are God-created parts—parts that are simultaneously the whole. *For the separation was simply an exaggeration of that part-ness at the expense of our oneness.* It was an act of withdrawing our intimate connectedness with the All, of retracting our total and inclusive extension and recoiling into ourselves as separate parts. It was the idea of part-ness taken to its ultimate extreme: totally separate and isolated parts, distinct and concrete, dependent on nothing but themselves, different from each other and alienated from the whole (see Diagrams 1A and 1B).

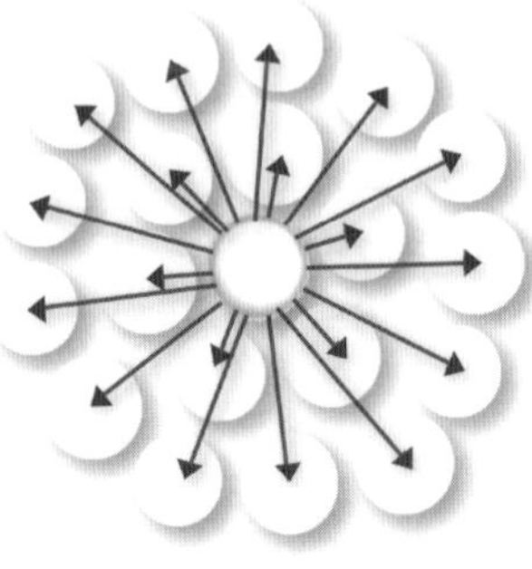

Diagram 1A
Oneness of the Parts

Diagram 1B
Part-ness over Oneness

In fact, the separation—even an *illusory* separation—is unthinkable without us already being parts in some slight, subtle sense, for it is this subtle part-ness that gave the separation its initial toehold. Without being in some sense a part among other parts, how would it have ever occurred to us to become a *special* part, a part competing with other parts for God's Love? This thought of specialness started the snowball rolling of exaggerating our part-ness at the expense of our oneness. This oneness was so natural and fundamental that the process took literally "millions of years" to complete (T-2.VIII.2:5). Yet when it was complete we were totally fixated on our part-ness and utterly blind to our oneness. We had transferred our focus from connectedness to isolation; we had substituted "fragmentation for wholeness" (T-18.I.4:2). This was a complete reversal of our beginning condition, in which our oneness vastly overshadowed our inconsequential, barely detectable part-ness.

What I am presenting here is a somewhat different interpretation than the fairly common idea among Course students that the single Son of God fell asleep, forming a massive primordial ego *which then* fragmented into different parts. What I am suggesting is that the single Son of God stayed awake, while pre-existing parts of the Son fell asleep due to the wish to be special and independent. My main reason for this is that I think the Course supports the latter view. The former view, to my knowledge, is based on what I consider to be a misreading of "The Substitute Reality" in Chapter 18 of the Text. This section does not say that a single primordial ego progressively fragmented, resulting in a multiplicity of individuals, but that the original error fragmented inside of our minds, resulting in our seemingly variable emotions and perceptions. Yet, of course, this is my interpretation. You will have to make up your own mind.

Psychological Separation

When we talk about the separation, it is easy to get a mental image of a little spark detaching and floating away from a vast expanse of undifferentiated light, heading off alone into the cold darkness of space. It is easy to envision the separation as an actual, physical separation (see Diagram 2A).Yet if we really could physically detach and travel away from Heaven (as if there were somewhere else to go), we would be in big trouble. At one point in the Course, Jesus tells us, "I am come to tell you that the choice of which is true [the world or God] is not yours to make. If it were, you would have destroyed yourself" (T-8.VI.2:4-5).

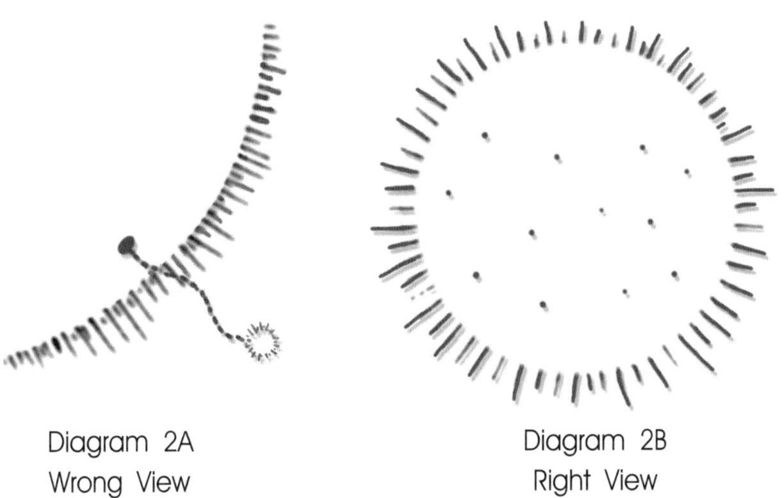

Diagram 2A
Wrong View

Diagram 2B
Right View

Rather than an actual, physical separation, the Course talks about it as a psychological separation. What is the difference? It is all the difference in the world. One is real, the other is only in the mind. It is the difference between seeing a real train speeding toward you, and *hallucinating* a train speeding toward you. One is going to smash you, the other is going to leave you unharmed, however much you anticipate being smashed. What Jesus is saying is that if the separation were real, we would have smashed ourselves.

Thus, it was a separation in consciousness, a dissociation. "We have said before that the separation was and is dissociation" (T-6.II.1:5). Dissociation, as defined by Webster's Dictionary is "the separation of an idea or activity from the mainstream of consciousness or of behavior esp. as a mechanism of ego defense." In other words, the primordial separation was the separation of God/Heaven/reality/oneness from the mainstream of consciousness as an ego defense.

Perhaps the best way to get a handle on this idea is to use three key psychological terms which are frequently used in the Course: *denial*, *insanity*, and *sleep*.

As we all know, denial as a psychological defense is where we choose to look the other way, to sweep something under the rug. The rug, of course, is our conscious mind. By sweeping something under consciousness we do not actually change anything. The thing that we are denying is still there and we are still aware of it. We are just no longer *consciously* aware of it.

The belief in separation was simultaneously a *denial* of oneness. In fact, it was a denial of everything true, including a denial of God: "[The god you made] has many forms, but although he may seem to be many different things he is but one idea;—the denial of God" (T-10.V.3:8). It was also a denial of our Self: "Deny your own Identity, and you assail the universe alone, without a friend, a tiny particle of dust against the legions of your enemies" (W-pI.191.3:2).

The separation, then, was a denial of the reality we knew to be true, the reality that was patently and transparently obvious to us, that we were in no way separate from, that we knew in direct, unmediated, permanent awareness. This denial did not change reality, nor even our awareness of reality. It just pushed it down in our minds, swept it under the rug. In fact, this act of pushing reality into unconsciousness *produced* the unconscious. Before that there was no such thing as hidden areas of our minds. There was only direct and naked awareness.

In our world, we have a word for the wholesale, across-the-board denial of reality. That word is "insanity." What do we normally mean when we say the word "insanity"? We generally mean a profound break with reality and a retreat into a strictly private, subjective world. This private world does not make sense; it does not reflect what is really out there. It is a twisted product of the insane person's own mind, a world that is real and meaningful only to him. His perceptions

> make up a private world that cannot be shared. For they are meaningful only to their maker, and so they have no meaning at all. In this world their maker moves alone, for only he perceives them. (T-13.V.1:7-9)

What we normally call insanity is a break with conventional, consensual physical and social reality. And only a minority of people seem to have done this. Yet all of us have had a profound break with true reality, transcendental reality. All of us have gone mad in Heaven. Reality remains exactly as it was. We just do not see it. We are still smack in the middle of Heaven, but we have gone so wildly insane that when we look outward we do not see the boundless oneness that actually surrounds us; we see a physical world of fragmented separateness.

Another analogy for what happened is falling asleep. Every day of our lives we experience a profound retreat from what we consider to be reality. We become unconscious of the world around us as we go into "the private world of sleep" (T-13.V.8:3). This, says the Course, is what happened to us in Heaven. We conked out, we became completely unaware of the reality that still surrounded us as we descended into our own private experience.

> The special ones are all asleep, surrounded by a world of loveliness they do not see. Freedom and peace and joy stand there, beside the bier on which they sleep, and call them to come forth and waken from their dream of death. Yet they hear nothing. They are lost in dreams of specialness. (T-24.III.7:1-4)

And, as with our current sleep, we not only lost awareness of reality, we lost awareness itself. Total awareness would necessarily mean awareness of totality, reality. To retreat from reality, then, we had to also retreat from awareness. All that remained was a faint fraction of awareness, a dim semi-consciousness—our current state. You may think that sleep implies complete unconsciousness. Yet sleep researchers have found that even in the deepest stages of sleep a subject when awakened will report having been in the middle of vague trains of dim thought. Could we ask for a more perfect analogy to our current condition?

As you can see, all three of these terms—denial, insanity and sleep—have a great deal in common. The place where these terms intersect reveals the real essence of the separation. They all paint a picture of the separation not as an objective occurrence, but as a psychological occurrence. To be more specific, all three terms suggest a mental retreat from reality, *a withdrawal from reality into the privacy of our own minds.* Even though reality remained totally unchanged, and on some level we remained aware of it, we lost consciousness of reality as we withdrew into the privacy of our minds. Reality did not change; only our perspective did. We did not leave; we simply fell into denial, went insane, fell asleep.

This was the separation, minds falling asleep in Heaven, withdrawing, closing in on themselves, exaggerating their part-ness at the expense of the allness. When you think of the separation, then, do not picture a little spark floating away from infinite light. Picture still an endless expanse of undifferentiated light. And then imagine that inside that light, implicit within it, are an infinite number of little lights, each one of them shining so brightly as to fuse completely with the light as a whole. Then imagine a large number of these little lights simply ceasing to shine, going dark, falling asleep. They do not go anywhere, they just shut their eyes momentarily, making tiny dark spots in the larger light (see Diagram 2B, p. 69).

This is a very crude visual analogy. But the idea behind it is crucial. We did not go anywhere. For there was nowhere to go. "To be alone is to be separated from infinity, but how can this be if infinity has no end? No one can be beyond the limitless, because what has no limits must be everywhere" (T-11.1.2:1-2). We could not change our nature. Our nature was out of our hands completely. It was God's creation and we simply had no say about it. "What God created is only what He would have it be, being His Will" (T-18.VI.5:5). We essentially accomplished nothing.

Like to the sun and ocean your Self continues, unmindful that this tiny part regards itself as you. It is not missing; it could not exist if it were separate, nor would the whole be whole without it. It is not a separate kingdom, ruled by an idea of separation from the rest [the ego]. Nor does a fence [the body] surround it, preventing it from joining with the rest, and keeping it apart from its Creator. This little aspect is no different from the whole, being continuous with it and at one with it. It leads no separate life, because its life *is* the oneness in which its being was created. (T-18.VIII.6)

Chapter 7
The Dreaming of the World

We have talked at length about our idea of becoming a separate part or entity. Yet the thought of separation entailed far more than a change in our understanding of self. As the Course points out in many different forms, any belief adopted by the mind cannot be completely compartmentalized, but will generalize and influence the entire mind, coloring its whole understanding of reality. For "it is impossible to fragment the mind" (T-7.VIII.4:2); "all commitments the mind makes are total" (T-7.VI.5:2). This is especially true of thoughts about self. For self-perception is the root of all perception. It is a basic psychological law in the Course that self-perception leads to perception of reality; self-concept leads to world view.

As a result, our "tiny, mad desire to be separate, different and special" (T-25.I.5:5), though seemingly directed solely at our own nature, actually took aim at much more than that. It was, in fact, an attack on every single aspect of reality: a substitution of separation for oneness, change for eternity, limitation for infinity, partiality for wholeness, pain for joy, hate for love, war for peace, guilt for innocence, uncertainty for knowledge, etc., etc., etc. It was obviously an attack on our brothers, for in requesting to be the special recipient of God's Love we were asking that they receive less. And, perhaps above all, it was an attack on God as our Authority, as Supplier of our needs, as our Father, and our Eternal Love.

As you can see, the idea of attack is at the core of the separation. Separation itself is an attack, an attempt to "break away a part of God Himself and thus destroy His Wholeness" (W-pI.132.13:1). Separation attacks the whole through the attempt to abandon or divorce the whole—seemingly ripping away part of it, leaving the whole wounded, lonely and incomplete. And it also attacks the whole by violating the very principle of wholeness or oneness. In fact, the Course says that the belief in separation

> *is* the 'devil.' It is powerful, active, destructive and clearly in opposition to God, because it literally denies His Fatherhood. Look at your life and see what the devil has made. (T-3.VII.5:1-3)

The "Shattering" of Heaven

Because the thought of separation was an attack thought that (like all thoughts) had to generalize, had to be projected outward, you can only imagine the effects it appeared to have—something like a celestial version of lighting one match and watching the whole forest go up in flames. The thought of separateness seemed to spread out from our minds like a giant shock wave roaring across a frozen lake, breaking up the seamless whiteness into billions of splintered fragments as it went. It seemed to explode the unity of Heaven into countless disconnected pieces, to "reduce [reality] to a little pile of unassembled parts" (W-pI.136.2:3), to "shatter knowledge into meaningless bits of disunited perceptions" (T-18.I.5:6).

> What is the world except a little gap perceived to tear eternity apart, and break it into days and months and years? And what are you who live within the world except a picture of the Son of God in broken pieces, each concealed within a separate and uncertain bit of clay?
> (T-28.III.7:4-5)

It looked like we had taken a wrecking ball to Heaven. Imagine the experience of sitting in the chaotic rubble of what had been Heaven—and all of it due to one tiny little idea. It was as if a child who had dearly loved and deeply cherished his home, spoke one tiny unkind word to his parents and watched it all—his parents, his house and his whole world—immediately explode into a cloud of glittering fragments. What do you think the child would be feeling at this point? What do you think *we* were feeling at this point?

The Course seems to say that we were feeling two things: the horror of guilt over the separation and the desire to protect and reinforce the separation—a tragic combination if ever there was one. Let us take these two reactions one at a time.

Guilt

Recall that the separation was an attack on reality, its members, and its Creator. And we believed that this attack was truly successful, that it really did shatter Heaven, fragment Christ, and mortally wound God. If this was true, what better word for this than "sin"? When would the word "sin" be more acutely and precisely appropriate than in this very situation? "To sin would be to violate reality, and to succeed. Sin is the proclamation that attack is real and guilt is justified" (T-19.II.2:2-3).

In other words, if we really did attack reality and succeed in violating it, then we sinned. And not just a little. We sinned big-time, mortally, fatally, spectacularly. And if we sinned, we are guilty. We have corrupted our soul, we have a "rusted core" (W-pI.133.10:1). And now we deserve to be punished for our sin, to be attacked and violated in return. The guilt that we carry from the original separation must be absolutely unimaginable. And it is lying within each one of us at this moment.

This guilt seems to be a fair, objective reaction to a truly destructive act. It seems to be a justified self-beating. Yet there is something fishy about it. For, as we saw in the last chapter, we cannot really attack reality. It is changeless, invulnerable. It cannot *be* violated. Guilt, then, is not an objective reaction to a transparently obvious occurrence. It is an act of self-deception. It is an affirmation that something happened that did not really happen.

Further, guilt is not a healthy motivator that moves us to be holy. Its actual effect is to *reinforce* attack. For guilt is the affirmation that attack is real, that it is not just a harmless mistake, but a mortal sin; and that because of it, attack on ourselves is now justified. Guilt makes attack real, and what has been made real has been reinforced.

Indeed, the Course sees guilt as the first and most basic reinforcement for the reality of the ego, since, as we saw, the idea of attack is at the heart of the ego. In fact, according to the Course, without our reaction of guilt to the initial tiny, mad idea, the separation would have immediately evaporated.

> Into eternity, where all is one, there crept a tiny, mad idea, at which the Son of God remembered not to laugh [in other words, instead of laughing he felt guilty]. In his forgetting did the thought become a serious idea, and possible of both accomplishment and real effects. Together, we can laugh them both away, and understand that time cannot intrude upon eternity. It is a joke to think that time can come to circumvent eternity.
>
> (T-27.VIII.6:2-5)

In other words, instead of feeling guilty, we should have just laughed. For attack can have no real effects. It is therefore crazy, but harmless—like all the things we laugh at. Laughter is not only the appropriate response, it is the response that would have corrected the problem—by dispelling the apparent reality of it. Guilt, on the other hand, makes it all very serious and ultra-real. Guilt is a reinforcement mechanism. And that leads into our other reaction to the tiny, mad idea.

The Desire to Protect and Reinforce

The fact that we felt guilty in response to the separation implies that we did not like what we had done, that we somehow wished to undo it. Yet, as we just saw, guilt actually reinforced the separation. And so the full picture must be that even stronger than our dislike for what we had done was our *attraction* to it. More than anything else, we wanted to keep it, to hang on to it. For had we only disliked it, we would have chosen to laugh it away. But instead we chose to feel guilty, which allowed us to turn our noses up at the separation in a way that would simultaneously express our attraction to it and reinforce it.

Why would we want to reinforce it? I think for two reasons. On the "positive" end we were still looking for the "high" of being God's favorite son and of being our own father. On the negative end we had identified with the ego and were afraid that letting it go and rejoining the One meant letting go of existence and being annihilated: "You feel the fear of the destruction of your thought system upon you as if it were the fear of death" (T-3.VII.5:10).

This fear was highly exacerbated by the fact that somewhere inside we sensed that the separation did not really change anything. We sensed that the ego was not real, however much we wanted to make it real. We could tell that God did not fulfill our request to be special, that "God did not allow this to happen" (T-13.III.11:6). And so, "While the ego is...unaware of spirit, it does perceive itself as being rejected by something greater than itself" (T-4.II.8:8).

Here, then, is the situation: we thought that we had separated from reality, leaving it in broken pieces. And our main investment was in reinforcing this separation. Yet at the same time we could dimly feel that God was still there, unchanged and unfragmented; that He was still just as non-special and impartial—and every bit as real—as before. We could tell that God's formless oneness loomed near, waiting to vaporize our separateness with its blinding brilliance. We feared if we came face to face with Him that His Love would crush us into nothingness (T-13.III.4:1), that His ocean would swallow our tiny ripple, His sun devour our little sunbeam (T-18.VIII.3:6).

This made our separation seem exceedingly precarious. What to do? We had to do something that would prove our separation to be real, something that would shut out God's deadly, marauding oneness for good.

Reversal of Cause and Effect

To protect the separation we had to hide its vulnerable insubstantiality. If it remained exposed to the light of day, that light would reveal it to be a vacuous illusion. We had to disguise it, make it seem like something it wasn't. We had to accomplish two things:

1. We had to make the idea of separation appear to not be our own invention, to not be an idea in our minds alone, one that we caused and that we could relinquish.
2. We had to make the idea of separation seem to be reality itself, a reality that was prior to us, that has power over us, that actually caused us.

In other words, in our minds we had to completely reverse cause and effect. We forgot that we were the cause of the separation-idea and instead imagined that it was its own cause. And then we went one step further and imagined that it in turn caused us, that separation is an independently existing reality that has power to hurt us or make us happy, even power to create us. "Effect and cause are first split off, and then reversed, so that effect becomes a cause; the cause, effect" (T-28.II.8:8).

This was the perfect protection, you must admit. How did we accomplish this? The clue lies in our trio of psychological terms for separation: denial, insanity and sleep. Fascinatingly, all three of these terms have a companion term. Once we *deny*, we support that denial with *projection*. Once we go *insane*, we start to *hallucinate* our own reality. And once we go to *sleep*, we begin to *dream*. In all three cases, then, we first shut down to reality and withdraw into the privacy of our minds. And then we project that private reality outward.

In other words, we protected our separation thought with the dynamic of projection. Projection is perfect for this job. In fact, this kind of thing is what it is made for. Projection takes an inner idea that we caused and throws it outside, making it appear to be an external force that causes us. This was the origin of the external world in which we seem to live. We projected it. Let us now look more closely at the process of making the world.

The Making of the World

Let us go back to the initial tiny, mad idea. The "first projection of error outward" (T-18.I.6:1) was what we described earlier, the projection of separation onto the whole of Heaven, seemingly "shatter[ing] knowledge into meaningless bits of disunited perceptions" (T-18.I.5:6). After that came the projection of the physical world. That projection seems to be talked about on two different levels in the Course. One level describes how we experienced making the world; the other level explains what was actually happening. I will attempt to recount them in that order.

If you recall, after the first projection of the tiny, mad idea, we found ourselves seemingly sitting among the chaotic rubble of what had been Heaven. What do we do now? We have already established that we want to build our own world, and, coincidentally enough, here we are surrounded by free building materials. The next step is academic. We simply start sifting through the rubble, picking and choosing which parts of Heaven that we like and which parts we don't. We do this by using our judgment: "Judgment…separates segments of reality by the unstable scales of desire" (T-3.VI.11:4). And then, having all of the parts around us that we really prefer, we start to build a world out of them. We arrange and organize them, attach one to another, add a part here and a part there. It is "a continual process of accepting and rejecting, organizing and reorganizing, shifting and changing" (T-3.V.7:7). And finally we end up with our own cosmos.

> The ego...is left with a series of fragmented perceptions which it unifies on behalf of itself. This, then, becomes the universe it perceives. (T-11.V.15:2-3)

If this makes the world sound like some sort of cosmic junk sculpture, that is no accident. For that is exactly how the Course talks about it. It says, "He does not realize he picked a thread from here, a scrap from there, and wove a picture out of nothing" (T-24.V.2:3). Elsewhere, we are told that it is a world "made of little bits of glass, a piece of wood, a thread or two, perhaps" (T-28.V.6:2).

This is certainly a simplistic way of talking about a process that must be beyond our current comprehension. Yet this process is not an irrelevant fossil from the beginning of time. It is one that we perform right now, in every minute of our lives. We are constantly involved in 1) mentally dividing things into separate parts; 2) selecting which parts we want to keep; and 3) organizing the preferred parts into a whole of our own making. More than once, in fact, the Course points out that we do this with the people in our lives. First, we see the Sonship fragmented into individual people. Then we select certain people, certain aspects of the Sonship, that we want to spend our time with. We even select particular body parts and personality characteristics that we really like on those people. And finally, we organize all the preferred parts, and parts of parts, into our own whole, our own personal world, our "life." "Thus does [the ego] assemble reality to its own capricious liking, offering for your seeking a picture whose likeness does not exist" (T-15.V.7:2).

The really odd thing about building the world out of the material of Heaven is that it required systematically distorting the real nature of that material. First, we separated out the parts, although in fact the parts were joined. Then we chose among the parts, which assumed they were truly different and unequal; though in fact they were identical and equal. Finally, we arranged them into a whole, putting each part in relationship with only a few other parts—a relationship that was partial at that. Yet, in truth, each part had a total relationship with every part and with the whole. As the Course says, it is a process that "takes fragments of the whole, assembles them without regard to all their true relationships, and thus constructs illusions of a whole that is not there" (W-pI.136.6:1).

This whole process is obviously a fiction. How could we splinter unchangeable Wholeness? How could we select among parts that are eternally joined? How could we construct a whole that was a complete violation of the true Whole? The answer is that we could not. And so none of that actually happened. We may have experienced it as a real process of separating, selecting and organizing, but in actuality it was pure projection, mere hallucination. The shock wave I described that broke Heaven up into fragments was simply the wave of our mind's projection, breaking Heaven up *in our perception*, not in truth. Onto those "broken" parts we then projected our belief that they were not only separate, but different and unequal, of different shapes, sizes, and varying degrees of significance and desirability. And then onto the same parts we projected our preferred arrangement, the way we wanted them to fit together.

All the while the parts remained exactly as they were: completely at one with each other, the same as each other, and identical to the whole. Nothing had happened to them. We just *saw* them as disassembling, being selected from and then reassembling. It was all in our minds. It was our own dream.

This tells us what you are looking at when you look out at your world. Each object—be it a rock, a machine, a building, a tree, an animal, or a human—is really a fragment of Heaven *falsely perceived.* It is one of your ancient heavenly brothers. Onto this formless part of eternal light you project a form, a mask, which makes it appear to be a unique, limited shape with its own distinctive nature. "By this you carve it out of unity" (W-pI.184.1:4). And, of course, it has donned the same mask in its mind. Thus, you and this brother have entered into a cooperative dance of illusions. "And thus his unity is twice denied, for you perceive him separate from you, and he accepts this separate name as his" (W-pI.184.8:7). Yet unbeknownst to you and to him, he remains a part of the "still infinity of endless peace" (T-29.V.2:4), unseparated, formless, and changeless.

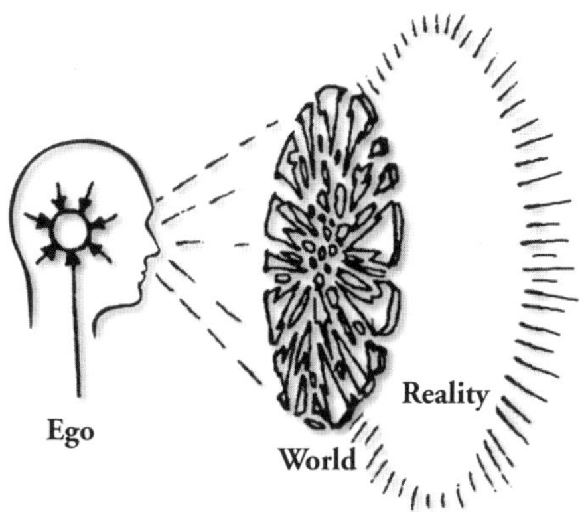

Diagram 3A
Projection of the World

In other words, we made the world by mentally superimposing form onto the formless. We projected separation onto oneness (see Diagram 3A). This world, then, is simply the ego-belief blown up into a whole environment, an entire cosmos. In one sweep this explains a great deal about the world. For its entire basis is the idea of separation. It is separation simply repeated over and over and over again, in every body, every cell, every molecule, atom and even subatomic particle. Space itself, the very matrix in which physical reality exists, is a projection of the idea of separateness. Space is distance; distance is separation. Space, as was said in Part I, is a realm in which everything is separate, a "world in which the proof of separation seems to be everywhere" (T-19.III.7:3).

In space, not only is there distance between every mind and every other mind, but each mind is enclosed in a body, a wall, a boundary. We made the body, like the world, to make separation real. And the body is absolutely key in this whole attempt. It is a simply unbeatable device for "proving" the reality of separation. It does this in at least two ways.

First, the body "proves" separation by enclosing us in its bubble, shut off from the rest of reality. "Each body seems to house a separate mind, a disconnected thought" (T-18.VIII.5:2). The body seems to be the cause of our separateness. Separation appears to be enforced on us by the body, rather than chosen by the mind. And that is exactly how we want it to appear.

Second, the body "proves" separation through its senses. It not only encloses us in its prison, the only windows in this prison look out onto more prisons, more bodies. Put more plainly, while we think we are in a body, we will believe that any news about a reality beyond our private mind must come through the body, through its senses, its eyes, and ears. And the only "reality" that those senses can sense is the world of bodies. The only news they broadcast is physical.

Just as space is a projection of the idea of separateness, time is a projection of the idea of change. Time and space go hand in hand. Space is fragmentation superimposed onto infinity, making infinity seem to be endlessly divided and subdivided into separate locations. Time is fragmentation superimposed onto eternity, making eternity appear to be broken up into a long string of separate moments. To return to a passage quoted earlier, time is "a little gap perceived to tear eternity apart, and break it into days and months and years," and space is "a picture of the Son of God in broken pieces, each concealed within a separate and uncertain bit of clay" (T-28.III.7:4-5).

The world of time and space, then, is extremely convincing evidence for the fundamental idea of the separation: the idea of fragmentation—of separate, independent parts, torn from the web of total relationship and wrenched from the innocence of complete dependency on God. Yet this is just the beginning. The world witnesses to far more than this.

Projection of Guilt

Recall that guilt was our first and foremost reinforcement for the reality of separation. Therefore, if the world is meant to witness to the thought of separation, then the world should also witness to the thought of guilt. And that is exactly what the Course says. In some profound and literal way, this world is a manifestation of guilt. The thought of separation gave the world its fundamental structure, but the thought of guilt is what gave it its *character*.

Recall that the beginning of the separation was our affirmation of separateness, which was simultaneously a denial of reality, pushing our awareness of reality down in our minds. To support this denial, we projected separateness outward, first seemingly fragmenting Heaven and then organizing a world of separateness out of those fragments.

This entire process from start to finish produced massive, intolerable guilt. And so we repeated the process of denial and projection. We denied our guilt, hiding it in our unconscious mind. And then we projected it outward. This projection seemed to expel guilt from our mind, relieving us of its burden. Yet our desire to get rid of our guilt was only the superficial motive for projecting it outward. Our deeper motive was our *attraction* to guilt, our need to protect and reinforce it, since guilt reinforces the separation. Projection satisfied both motives, for in throwing our guilt outside of us, it both *seemingly* got rid of it and *actually* reinforced it—by transforming it from our own subjective idea into an objective, external reality.

Think of it in this way. To feel guilt, your mind must play two roles at once. There must be a defendant part of your mind, a part of your mind that has committed some kind of crime. And there must be a judge part of your mind, a part that looks on the crime and declares the defendant guilty.

In projecting our guilt, as we said, our surface motive is to escape it. And so we project the defendant part of ourselves outward, retaining the role of judge for ourselves. The guilty, "evil" part of us seems to be outside of us now, and we seem to be the innocent judge—upright, clean, and in a position to pass sentence. This results in a world perceived as cruel, evil, murderous, and a self perceived as righteous and innocent. This kind of projection is largely responsible for our conscious experience of the world. For our daily experience is one of standing back and judging the world for its despicable sins while feeling relatively innocent ourselves. This approach works superficially, yet ultimately it backfires, because now we see a dangerous criminal out there ready to rob, rape, or murder us. And, even more to the point, we feel guilty for judging him, for condemning him as a criminal, because that condemnation is an attack.

So projecting the defendant outward results in more guilt. Obviously our underlying attraction to guilt is at play here. Yet this attraction is even more destructive, for what it mainly does is lead us to project the *judge* outward and retain the role of the defendant. Just hearing this should send shivers up our spine. For now when we look out at the world, we see a cruel, pitiless and immovable judge gazing relentlessly right at our blackest sins, pronouncing sentence on us to the full extent of the law and handing us over to the executioner (see Diagram 3B).

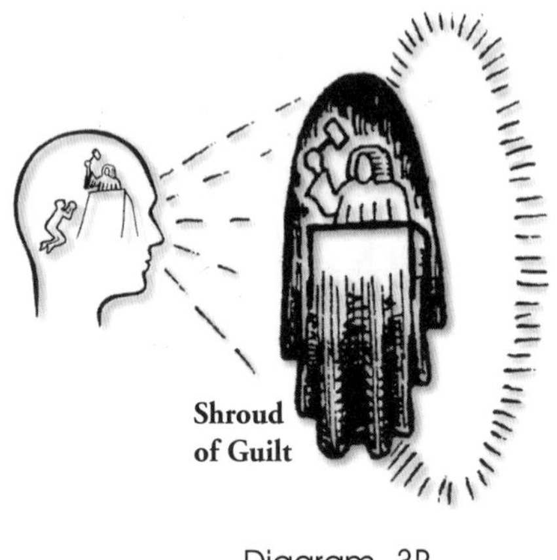

Diagram 3B
Projecting the World

If we really wanted to reinforce our guilt, this is exactly what we would do. We would imagine that all of reality believed in our guilt. Now our guilt seems no longer to be our own subjective theory. It is the considered and venerated opinion of the entire world. Now *that* is how to make guilt real.

And whereas projecting the defendant gave rise to our conscious experience of the world, projecting the judge gives rise to the actual laws by which the world works. This latter projection is the deeper one, and thus is far more unconscious. Therefore, whereas it is relatively apparent why we blame the world so much, we have no idea why the world attacks *us* so incessantly. We all know that the world attacks us. But we do not know why. Yet if this is our dream, there can be only one rational answer: *this world is so attacking because it is being dreamt out of our belief that we deserve to be attacked.* We have dreamt a world of punishment to confirm our belief that we *deserve* to be punished. And that belief is guilt.

The Course, therefore, is making the unique (to my knowledge) and nearly unbelievable statement that the world is a manifestation of guilt. The world was made to punish us and thus prove the validity of our guilt. All its difficulties, all its limits, its frustrations, injustices, disasters, tragedies, and wars add up to one vast dream of punishing ourselves for our sins. That is why life here is so hard. That is why the world is so incredibly attacking, why everything in the world is under assault, constantly besieged by a host of factors surrounding it, "attacked by armies massed against itself" (W-pI.96.5:3), "a tiny particle of dust against the legions of [its] enemies" (W-pI.191.3:2). The world, in fact, is one big attack machine. Yet, strangely, all of this "outer" attack is simply a dream of self-punishment:

> Like to a dream of punishment, in which the dreamer is unconscious of what brought on the attack against himself, he sees himself attacked unjustly and by something not himself. He is the victim of this "something else," a thing outside himself, for which he has no reason to be held responsible. He must be innocent because he knows not what he does, but what is done to him. Yet is his own attack upon himself apparent still, for it is he who bears the suffering. And he cannot escape because its source is seen outside himself. (T-27.VII.1:3-7)

There is a very powerful passage in the Course that makes it absolutely clear that from its standpoint the physical—atomic, chemical, and biological—world is a manifestation of guilt:

> The world you see is the delusional system of those made mad by guilt. Look carefully at this world, and you will realize that this is so. For this world is the symbol of punishment, and all the laws that seem to govern it are the laws of death. Children are born into it through pain and in pain. Their growth is attended by suffering, and they learn of sorrow and separation and death. Their minds seem to be trapped in their brain, and its powers to decline if their bodies are hurt. They seem to love, yet they desert and are deserted. They appear to lose what they love, perhaps the most insane belief of all. And their bodies wither and gasp and are laid in the ground, and are no more. Not one of them but has thought that God is cruel. (T-13.In.2:2-11)

In other words, the basic physical and biological facts of bodily encasement—birth, childhood, limitation, vulnerability, loss, aging and death—make us suffer. They *attack* us and so are dream symbols of our belief that we deserve attack. The world, therefore, is a massive dream symbol of guilt.

To underscore the literalness of this, the Course includes a significant passage about the dreaming of the world. This passage, in the section, "The Two Worlds" (T-18.IX), sketches the following basic scenario: Deep, deep down in our minds is our guilt. Just above that guilt lies "the circle of fear" (4:1). In this circle lies the full fury of our attack thoughts, of murder, vengeance, and betrayal. These thoughts are disguised manifestations of our guilt, designed "to keep the guilt in place" (4:2), to confirm and hide it. Out of this circle of fear then rises the physical world, whose purpose is to disguise the disguise, to doubly hide the guilt and keep it from being examined and relinquished. The world, then, is simply shapes rising and falling, standing and moving about in the "clouds of guilt" (8:1).

Death

The final purpose of the world's attack on us is our death. Our guilt is so great, we feel, that the only penalty of which we are truly deserving is the death penalty. As the Bible says, "The wages of sin is death."

As a result, this world is summarized by the idea of death. "This world *is* a picture of the crucifixion of God's Son" (T-13.In.4:1). Every life, no matter how vibrant with hopes and dreams, must end in death. "It is the one fixed, unchangeable belief of the world that all things in it are born only to die" (M-27.1:4). And while things live, they live off of the death of other things. "And so do all things live because of death. Devouring is nature's 'law of life'" (M-27.3:6-7).

Being the natural outcome of guilt, death is seen to be the ultimate power in this world. "For it seems to hold all living things within its withered hand; all hopes and wishes in its blighting grasp; all goals perceived but in its sightless eyes" (W-pI.163.2:2). Indeed, death seems to be the ultimate power in all of reality, stronger even than God Himself. Any kind of lessening or limiting of life is the idea of death. And that is all we have seen from the very start of the separation. We have seen a picture in which the boundless life of Heaven is fractured into little, limited pieces that are lacking and empty, that can be attacked, injured, drained of life and joy, and finally killed. This world, then, is a picture of death, based on the belief that we deserve to die.

A World of Fear

To summarize: first we adopted the ego, the belief in separation. Then we projected this belief in separation outward, seemingly fragmenting Heaven and then reorganizing it into the physical world. Then, over the basic structure of separateness, we threw the dark shroud of our guilt, making the world appear to be guilty, sinful and evil; and yet deeper than that, making the world a massive penal system bent on our apprehension, conviction, imprisonment, and, finally, death.

Using projection we reversed cause and effect. The belief in separation, nothing more than the isolated effect of our minds, was seemingly thrown outside of us and now seemed to be reality itself. Now it was our cause; we were its effect, its slaves, offspring in its nest, guests in its home, strangers in its land. Now it had complete power over us, power to tell us what to do and what to feel, power to tell us what is real, to dictate to us our own nature—to tell us who we are. It seemed to be the dreamer, and we the dream, a puppet on its string, "a dancing shadow, leaping up and down according to a senseless plot conceived within the idle dreaming of the world" (T-27.VII.8:7).

This is an extremely fearful situation. For the world we live in is literally made of the power of our own mind turned against us and thrown outside us. There, it seems to ring us about with enemies bent on our destruction, intent on punishing us until we finally expire. In short, we seem to be the sad victims of the world, a very violent, cruel, fearful world, "a world of murder and attack, through which you thread your timid way through constant dangers, alone and frightened, hoping at most that death will wait a little longer before it overtakes you and you disappear" (T-20.III.4:1-2).

Yet this fear is all a ruse. For, "*You made this up*. It is a picture of what you think you are; of how you see yourself" (T-20.III.4:3-4). What we fear is what we are doing to ourselves. "Thus does he fear his own attack, but sees it at another's hands" (T-28.II.7:7). "What he beholds is his own fear external to himself, poised to attack, and howling to unite with him again" (W-pI.161.8:2). In other words, the world of fear is nothing but a trick we are playing on ourselves, a massive charade to keep ourselves from awakening.

Chapter 8
Reflections on the Nature of the World

Hopefully the last chapter gave you some appreciation for the fact that the Course is presenting a very different view of the world than what we are accustomed to. This jarring difference raises the question, "Just how literally are we supposed to take this picture?" Personally, I have no question that the Course intends it to be taken very literally indeed. It really means that all things in time and space are dream images of separation, all the way down to the atomic level and all the way out to the galactic level. It really means that the laws of nature are manifestations of a cosmic, primordial guilt. It really means that our own external problems are unconscious self-punishment.

On a literal level, my personal guess is that the process of making the world went something like this. As the Course mentions, the process of separating "occurred over millions of years" (T-2.VIII.2:5). I think that with extreme gradualness our minds fell into the belief in separation. And with each stage of that belief came a corresponding projection. In other words, when we believed in separation just a hair, our minds projected just a hint of form onto the formlessness of Heaven. As we bought into separation more, our minds projected a little more form. In this way, I think we gradually dreamt into place one plane at a time (I am talking about the nonphysical planes of occult lore). First came the highest plane, beautiful, radiant, with just the slightest, subtlest hint of form; similar to Heaven, but definitely not Heaven. As our minds went a little crazier, we dreamt the next plane down, and so on. Down it went, through what are commonly called the causal plane, the subtle plane, and the astral plane. Each time we fell more deeply asleep we dreamt a realm of harder boundaries, harsher punishment, and greater fear.

Finally, we just passed out completely and dreamt this place, the physical universe, as a dream of extreme separateness and merciless punishment. Thus, the big bang that began this universe fifteen billion years ago was a distant echo of the original separation. As with all of the other dream realms, the forms of this new realm—large or small, micro- or macroscopic—were dream images. Its "laws"—of physics, chemistry, and biology—were dream rules, and its events dream symbols, symbolizing the core beliefs in separation, attack, sin, guilt, and death. This universe, then, was a deeper dream. And, who knows, there may be deeper dreams still.

Thus, I really do think that the Course is absolutely literal in talking about the world as a dream. In this chapter I would like to spend some time reflecting on the Course's view of the world, in the form of sketching its main points and in doing just a little comparison between this new view and more traditional views.

1. The World Is the Product of Our Own Minds

There is no outside force that is responsible for the world, not God and not mindless physical forces. The world is a strictly psychological product. It is projection, an hallucination, a dream. Because of this, when we (all of us) stop mentally supporting it, it will be gone, without a trace, just as a mental image is gone once we stop imaging it: "The stars will disappear...and the sun...will vanish" (T-17.II.4:1). Our mental support is literally the only thing holding it up. The world will end in the exact same way that a dream ends when one awakens. "It will not be destroyed nor attacked nor even touched. It will merely cease to seem to be" (M-14.2:11-12).

2. The World Is the Outpicturing of Our State of Mind

As with any dream or hallucination, "The world you see...is the witness to your state of mind, the outside picture of an inward condition" (T-21.Intro.1:2,5). As we saw in the last chapter, the Course is saying that the world is essentially a dream symbolizing the belief in separation, attack, sin, guilt, death, etc.

> The world you see is a vengeful world, and everything in it is a symbol of vengeance. Each of your perceptions of "external reality" is a pictorial representation of your own attack thoughts. One can well ask if this can be called seeing. Is not fantasy a better word for such a process, and hallucination a more appropriate term for the result? (W-pI.23.3)

3. The World Is an Illusion

The Course is emphatic that the world is not real. It is literally not there. "There is no world!" (W-pI.132.6:2).

> What if you recognized this world is an hallucination? What if you really understood you made it up? What if you realized that those who seem to walk about in it, to sin and die, attack and murder and destroy themselves, are wholly unreal? (T-20.VIII.7:3-5)

To clarify this, I think it is the forms of the world that are completely unreal. Behind each form there is, I believe, something truly real. Behind each human body, animal body, plant body and even rock body is a son of God. Yet this son of God is not a form. He is a formless reality in Heaven, a seamless part of the whole. He merely dreams that he is a form. And we, in telepathic agreement with him, project onto him more or less the same form. In other words, we are projecting form onto the formless, much like projecting movie images onto the blank whiteness of the movie screen. The forms that we see, then, are not so much illusions as *hallucinations*.

4. The World Is a Denial of Reality, the Opposite of Reality

Being a projection of our insane denial of reality, "this world *is* the opposite of Heaven, being made to be its opposite, and everything here takes a direction exactly opposite of what is true" (T-16.V.3:6). The initial tiny, mad idea was so insane, so contrary to reality, that it had to produce a world that was directly opposite to reality.

> You may be surprised to hear how very different is reality from what you see. You do not realize the magnitude of that one error. It was so vast and so completely incredible that from it a world of total unreality had to emerge. What else could come of it? (T-18.I.5:1-4)

Initially it can be very shocking to read a statement like the following: "The world was made as an attack on God" (W-pII.3.2:1). Yet upon reflection it can become not only profound, but deeply appropriate. I recall one day being out driving, looking at the small, gnarled trees, dead grasses and cacti that dot the landscape of my area. I was thinking about how everything I see is limited; how everything is struggling to stay alive, locked in combat over the same limited resources; and how everything I see will die. My feeling was: What could this world be but one big mass of minds that have inwardly turned their back on infinite love and happiness? In short, what could the world be but resistance to the goodness of God?

This is not to say that the world is nothing but hate, pain, conflict, and death. Of course there is love and joy in this world. As the Course says, "Not even what the Son of God made in insanity could be without a hidden spark of beauty" (T-17.II.5:5). Yet, let's face it, that spark is pretty hidden. The honest love in this world is far and away overshadowed by the duplicity, pettiness, and misery. As such, the world deserves the label of being opposite to Heaven. From Heaven's standpoint, the world must look downright bizarre, as the following poignant passage suggests:

> This is the anti-Christ; the strange idea there is a power past omnipotence, a place beyond the infinite, a time transcending the eternal....Here the deathless come to die, the all-encompassing to suffer loss, the timeless to be made the slaves of time. Here does the changeless change; the peace of God, forever given to all living things, give way to chaos. And the Son of God, as perfect, sinless and as loving as his Father, come to hate a little while; to suffer pain and finally to die.
>
> (T-29.VIII.6:2-6)

5. The World Is a Psychological Defense Against Reality

Let's face it, if the world was made to prove that separateness, guilt, and attack are real and that oneness, innocence, and love are false, it works pretty darn well. It surely has convinced all of us. After a lifetime on planet Earth, truly believing in perfect, boundless, changeless love is an act of supreme and heroic faith. Believing in a God of love is a feat for a mental gymnast. Believing that we are infinite beings rather than *homo sapiens* is nearly impossible. As a defense, the world works. It

> "proves" God's Son is evil; timelessness must have an end; eternal life must die. And God Himself has lost the Son He loves, with but corruption to complete Himself, His Will forever overcome by death, love slain by hate, and peace to be no more. (W-pII.4.3:3-4)

6. The World Is Inside of Our Minds

One of the more startling implications of the fact that the world is a psychological construct is the idea that it is within our minds, where all our psychological constructs are. When you dream, where is your dream? As the Course says about dreams, "here is a world, clearly within your mind, that seems to be outside" (T-18.II.5:3). Hallucinations also may seem to be outside, but obviously they are images in the person's mind, images that have simply been labelled as external. The same with projections. The word "projection" conjures up an image of thoughts actually being beamed outside of our minds, like images from a movie projector. Yet that cannot be, for as the Course says, "Ideas leave not their source, and their effects but seem to be apart from them. Ideas are of the mind. What is projected out, and seems to be external to the mind, is not outside at all" (T-26.VII.4:7-9).

In other words, the projecting is only an internal process. Nothing actually leaves the mind. Projection, then, is simply a process whereby we take certain inner contents and label them "external," making what is inside seem to be outside.

Just as it is easy to envision the separation incorrectly as sparks of light actually leaving the greater light, so it is easy to picture the world and its relationship to Heaven incorrectly. I think we often picture the world being beamed out of our minds like a movie being beamed out of a projector. Perhaps we picture all of these sparks that have left Heaven floating together in space and beaming the world out of their minds (see Diagram 4A, p. 96).

Yet a more accurate picture would be this: as we said in Chapter 6, nothing has left Heaven. Some of its parts have simply fallen asleep while still in Heaven. They have retreated from reality into the privacy of their minds. And in the privacy of their minds they are dreaming.

The world is this dream, nothing more. It is simply a collection of images inside the dreaming minds (see Diagram 4B).

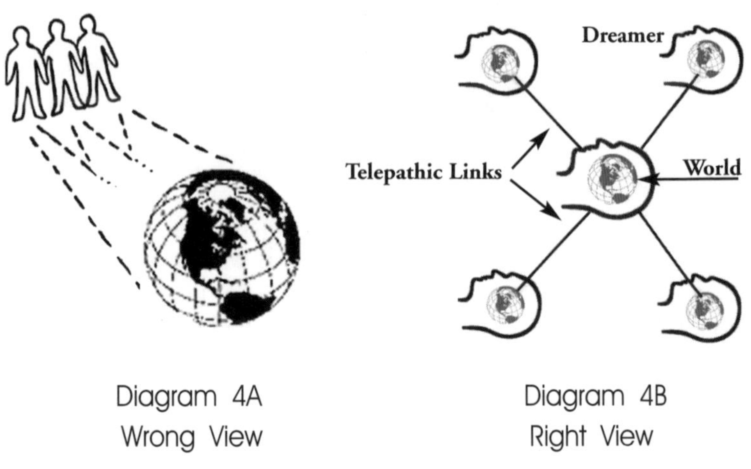

Diagram 4A
Wrong View

Diagram 4B
Right View

Other Views of the World

To my knowledge, the Course's view of the world is unique. Think about some of the standard, traditional images of the world. One, of course, is the Western religious image. In that view, a loving Creator creates the physical world. This world is real and God even declares it good. The Course would disagree on every point of this:

> The world you see is an illusion of a world. God did not create it, for what He creates must be eternal as Himself. Yet there is nothing in the world you see that will endure forever. (C-4.1:1-3)

We are so accustomed to the idea that God created the world. Yet, the funny thing is that it is the world itself—this supposed handiwork of God—that is probably the single biggest cause for lack of religious faith. The fact that there is so much suffering here, that evil seems so rampant and triumphant, that things seem to make so little sense, that God seems to be on a permanent lunch break—this is the stuff that makes atheists. Given the crazy nature of life here, I think it is easier to believe what the Course is saying, that the world is a psychological defense *against* God.

Another common view is the modern scientific view, which tends to see the world as self-existing and as the only reality. Mind or consciousness is a product of the physical world. The Course, on the other hand, sees mind as the only reality. The world, in its view, is an illusion, a product of mind. The world is one huge multifaceted dream symbol. All of its laws, structures, processes and events are shaped by mind to symbolize certain insane belief structures in the mind.

Another traditional view is the Hindu view that the world is an illusory manifestation of the Ground of being, Brahman. This comes closer to the Course's view in that it affirms the unreality of the world. Yet it also departs from the Course in making God the Source of the world. In one common Indian image, the universe is God's Divine *Lila* or Divine play. It emanates from Him. It is His dream.

The Course is saying that not only is the world an illusion, but its origin had nothing to do with God; it was not God-created. It was strictly the product of *parts* of God's Kingdom, parts of Heaven that fell into an insane denial of reality, while still in the middle of reality. As such, there is nothing objectively existing about this dream. It is a product of the mind and, in fact, is going on strictly inside of minds still in Heaven. It is our own dream, a dream designed to prove to us that Heaven is not true. Thus, it is a dream that symbolizes attack on God, attack on transcendental reality, attack on oneness, attack on our true nature. And it is a dream that symbolizes guilt; it is "a dream of punishment" (T-27.VII.1:3). As a whole package, I feel that this vision of the world is unique. And though it can seem depressing, it carries some unique and powerful spiritual benefits that will be discussed in Chapter 11.

Is the World a Collective or Individual Dream?

One question that often comes up is whether the world is a dream being dreamt by everyone, or if maybe I am dreaming it all by myself and all of you are just figures in my dream. As I see it, the world is a collective dream within which we are each projecting our own individual dream.

The Course is clear in saying that the world as a whole is a collective dream: "Even the mad idea of separation had to be shared before it could form the basis of the world I see" (W-pI.54.3:3). In other words, we dreamt up the physical world not just by ourselves, but in alliance with all separated minds, not only those parts of Heaven that have seemingly taken on a human form, but those that seem to be animals, plants, rocks, etc., and even those that have taken form in places besides this Earth.

Remember our picture of minds falling asleep in Heaven and dreaming the dream of the world inside themselves? To make this picture more complete, we must envision these minds as being in telepathic communication with each other and thus dreaming the same overall dream (see Diagram 4B, p. 96). This telepathic communication is a vestige of the total oneness that these minds truly share, but have temporarily forgotten.

It is as if a group of people fell asleep in a large room and began to dream. These people were telepathically linked, and so, through unconscious agreement, began to dream the same overall dream. Let's say they dreamt of being on the same field of battle, viewing and participating in the same events. It would be the same overall dream, but with one key difference: each one would dream of being a different character on that same field.

One result of this is the fact that the forms that we see, the events that we experience, and even the physical "laws" that seem to govern us are unconscious collective agreements. The world (as we have probably suspected all along) is a product of committee! Yet it is not the case that all minds have to convene and discuss each and every happening. Just as in our nighttime dreams where the unconscious seems to automatically project a symbolic picture of itself, so in our daytime dreams the collective unconscious does the same.

The best example that I know of for this kind of process is from an experiment done in the field of parapsychology. A group of people wanted to know if the startling phenomena that occur at seances were really the product of an actual discarnate spirit, or were merely produced by the group mind of the participants. To test this they invented their own fictional discarnate spirit. Then they conducted seances in which they summoned him. Spectacular things happened. One of the phenomena was table rapping, in which a spirit supposedly answers yes or no questions by causing loud popping noises to emanate from inside of the wood of the seance table. One rap for "yes," two for "no."

Yet what this group realized was that they, as a group, were unconsciously projecting the answers based on their memory and interpretation of the biography they had invented for the spirit. If they all assumed that the answer to a certain question would be "yes," they would get one rap. If they all assumed "no," they would get two raps. But if they were unclear, or if they were divided, they would get a garbled or uncertain result. The point is that their minds were causing the rapping based on collective agreement, an agreement that did not have to be openly discussed or polled. Whatever was strongest or clearest in the group thought-web simply manifested. This story, I think, is a powerful metaphor for the entire physical world, its basic structure and its mass events. The whole thing is just a massive tangle of dream symbols manifesting from collective unconscious agreement.

Yet, as I said, there is also a very powerful individual aspect to the dream. Each one of us is having our own individual dream in the midst of the collective dream. This individual dream has two aspects: internal and external.

First, we *internally* experience the collective dream according to our own personal set of attitudes and beliefs. We interpret the same outer happenings in our own individual way. The Course is very clear in saying that we do not see sanely what is right in front of our eyes. Instead we see and interact with memories from our past, which we project onto present events. We especially see and interact with our own "shadow figures"—memories of people who in our eyes did not give us the love we wanted. When someone talks to us in the present, then, we do not hear what he or she is saying. What we "hear" speaking to us is the shadow figure that we project onto that person. And it is to this shadow figure that we speak in response. In the middle of the collective dream, we are lost in our own private hallucination. Think about this. The normal definition of "insane" is someone who is seriously out of touch with consensual reality. "Consensual reality" is simply another term for the collective dream. And each one of us is seriously out of touch with the collective dream.

Second, even the *external* events that happen to us are the events that we personally dreamt into our experience:

> It is impossible the Son of God be merely driven by events outside of him. It is impossible that happenings that come to him were not his choice. (T-21.II.3:1-2)

This means that our car accidents, illnesses, unexpected blessings, and all the events that seem to come to us by chance are of the same nature as our dreams at night. Nighttime dreams and daytime dreams are both products of our own psyche. Painful or difficult outer circumstances, however, should not cause us to feel guilty. That is falling into the ego's trap, for we dream those difficulties into our lives for that very purpose: to punish ourselves and thus confirm our unconscious guilt.

The dream as a whole—the structure of physical "reality" and the mass events that occur—is a *collective* dream. Our own experience of it—our emotional reactions to it and our particular life events—is our own *individual* dream.

Why Is the Dream so Convincing?

It can be so extremely hard to believe that this world is a dream. And the reason should be clear by now: its function is to appear real. That is why we dreamt it. All dreams seem to be real while we are dreaming them. They seem to be external and independently existing, when in fact they are neither. Yet the dream of the physical world is far more convincing than our nighttime dreams. Why is that? There are many factors that seem to contribute to this convincing nature.

First, this dream, as we said, is collective. It is a group dream. We can be sure that the very reason we did not go off and dream our own dream, but instead invited all of our heavenly brothers to go in on it with us, was that their support made the dream seem far more real. In contrast, our nighttime dreams, which are private, are not nearly so convincing.

Second, the dream is unbelievably vast and intricate, as well as extremely consistent and persistent. It just seems too big and too complicated to come out of our own minds. And it is not full of the obvious irrationalities of nighttime dreams, where things shift and change for no rhyme or reason. And, unlike nighttime dreams, it keeps going; it never seems to end.

Third, we have lost touch with the reference point of reality. One reason that nighttime dreams are so obviously unreal is that we wake up from them every morning and can compare them with waking "reality."

Fourth, we have lost touch with the part of our minds that is generating the dream. We find it nearly impossible to consciously influence the dream with our minds alone. It thus seems completely independent of our minds and hence objectively real.

All four of these factors stem from one single thing: *we are dreaming the world out of an exceedingly deep part of our minds*. This part is so deep that we have forgotten about it. It is so deep that it is closer to our oneness with our brothers (thus the telepathic link that makes the dream collective). This same depth also makes it closer to the infinite power and intelligence of our true nature (thus the vastness, complexity, consistency, and persistence of the dream). In comparison, our puny nighttime dreams are coming from a place far closer to the surface. If you could liken our minds to the Earth, our nighttime dreams are coming from six inches underground and our daytime dream is coming from a place thousands of miles underground, just outside the Earth's molten core.

The reason that the dream of the physical world is coming out of such a deep part of our minds is that that is how deep our investment in illusions is. Therefore, this part of our minds, though invested with a greater intelligence, is invested in illusions with an unyielding fury that is almost beyond imagination. We very deeply want illusions to be true and Heaven to be false. This profound investment is what has shut out experience of the reference point of reality. And it is what has produced this world, which is such convincing "proof" for the unreality of Heaven. And when we actually start loosening up this investment, things will change. Physical "reality" will itself loosen up. Physical "laws" will start to be transcended, first a little and then dramatically. Then some of us will actually start to disappear from the dream, as Jesus did, as we let go of the ego and stop dreaming our bodies. Then, perhaps, whole planets will begin to vanish. And then, "The stars will disappear in light" (T-17.II.4:1), followed by galaxies and galactic clusters. And finally time/space itself will "merely cease to seem to be" (M-14.2:12).

Chapter 9
Nothing Has Happened

In terms of the separation, the Course is combining two seemingly incompatible ideas. On the one hand, the separation appears to be a literally cosmic drama, in which we ripped ourselves away from the wholeness of Heaven, demolished God's Kingdom, invented time and space and filled them with our own vast universe, and finally became voluntarily enslaved to this universe as our cause rather than our effect. On the other hand, the Course is telling us that no matter how immense this drama seems to be, it is not real; "*the separation never occurred*" (T-6.II.10:7). It is a basic Course principle that though we have complete power over our own experience, we have absolutely zero power over reality. For reality is changeless. No matter how hard we try, we cannot make a dent in it. No matter how heinous are the sins we seem to commit, reality—even our own reality—is unaffected.

Therefore, nothing happened. Nothing has changed. We are still in Heaven. We are still the perfect Sons of God. We are still resting in boundless peace, wrapped in our Father's Love. What changed was not reality itself, only our *experience* of it. This is simply another way of saying that separation was not God's idea, but was confined to the parts of the Sonship, initiated by those parts, participated in by them, and occurred only inside the privacy of their minds.

Yet how can this be? For it directly contradicts the current fact of our existence. It seems to be the most irrefutable fact that I am a human being, a separate entity living inside of a physical body, that I am firmly located inside of space and am passing through time. How can these seemingly basic pillars of my existence be completely false?

The answer lies in the power of the mind. We all know that the mind can believe in and experience things that are not true. We all know that the mind can play tricks on us, that we can deceive ourselves. In our psychologically sophisticated age, we are becoming increasingly aware that the mind is not simply observing objective reality; to some large degree it is manufacturing its own subjective reality. In fact, a basic dictum of the Course is that the mind can give itself an experience of whatever it thinks is real. Whatever reality the mind *believes* is real, that reality will the mind *experience* as real.

Let us, then, go through the basic pillars of our existence here and explore how they could seem true without actually *being* true.

How Can it Be That I Am Not Who I Think I Am?

The Course suggests that you are incredibly off in who you think you are. Who, then, is this "you"? For instance, when you say "I" in conversation, what do you mean? Well, I think you mean two things.

First, you mean this indefinable something, this thing that makes your choices, feels your feelings, thinks your thoughts, wills your actions, has your awareness, this thing that is you.

Second, you assume that you intimately know what this indefinable thing is. You have tacked onto this "I" a whole universe of qualities, traits, and characteristics. How you define this "I" at any given moment is shaped and molded by every single thing that has any connection to it whatsoever. Every thought you have, every feeling you experience, every word you say and action you perform, every word spoken to you and thing done to you, every person you associate with, every possession and dollar you own, every achievement you make, every thing from your past and every thing anticipated in your future—all of this colors who you think you are. All of it is just one more brush stroke on the canvas of your self-concept.

Yet you are just assuming that all of these things tell you something important and accurate about the "I" that makes your choices, thinks your thoughts, and feels your feelings. Given this, the really interesting thing is that you have never seen this "I." You have never seen yourself. This is so because you are in a condition of subject and object, in which the subject is always standing outside the object, perceiving the object, or acting upon it. The subject, then, is always the observer, never what is observed. It is always the seer, never what is seen.

Seeing the seer would be like trying to see your eyeball without a mirror. It can't be done, for, like the "I," the eye is what sees, not what is seen. Just as the eyeball cannot see itself, so you have never seen yourself. You have seen your body, your thoughts, your feelings, your sensations; but never the thinker, the feeler, the senser.

As a result, you could be anything. You could be completely different from the person you think you are. All of the things you have thought, felt, done, and experienced may tell you literally nothing correct about you, the experiencer, the doer.

But how is it that your thoughts, feelings, and choices could not be some roughly accurate reflection of you? The reason, again, is the power of the mind. No matter what the mind really is, when it adopts a certain belief about itself it will live up (or down) to that belief and will surround itself with evidence of the truth of that belief. We all know this principle. If you think you are a rotten person, you will think, speak and act like a rotten person. If you really believe in your ability to do something, you will draw out that ability. This principle can produce the most incredible results. Anorexics can believe so strongly in being overweight, that they can actually see a fat person in the mirror, even when they are deathly thin. There are stories of feral children, children who were raised by animals. These children so strongly believed they were animals that in every respect they behaved like animals, even to the point of running on all fours faster than a normal human could run on two legs.

The point is, once you plug a belief into the mind, the mind conforms itself to the belief entirely. The Course says, "Its [The mind's] direction is always automatic, because it cannot but be dictated by the thought system to which it adheres" (T-4.II.10:5). Putting a belief into the mind is like shining a white light through a colored slide. The light will take on the colors and contours of the slide perfectly. It is like giving an actor a script. The actor will seemingly become his character in the script. Or it is like putting a program into a computer. In each case you have an agent that will conform itself completely to a preset pattern. When the mind adopts and conforms itself to a belief, the mind gives the appearance, to itself and to others, of essentially *being* that belief. It thinks, it feels, it looks, and it acts just like that belief.

In other words, it *is* possible to be totally different than we seem to be. And that is exactly the case with us at present. As we saw in Part I we are eternal parts of the transcendental Christ. Each one of us is part of the Christ yet simultaneously and literally all of the Christ. Each one of us is a being as holy as Jesus, as holy as God. That is why the Course asks us to say to ourselves, "My mind is part of God's. I am very holy" (W-pI.35).

What has happened is that the parts that we are have adopted a crazy belief, the ego. We, limitless spirits in Heaven, have decided that we are tiny individual egos, encased in bodies. And, since minds always obey the beliefs they adopt, we now obey the ego-belief completely, flawlessly, perfectly. We think just like an ego. We feel ego-feelings. We make the choices that only an ego would make. We say the things at parties that only egos say at parties. We go around wearing a body, something only an ego would dream of doing. And we live in a place that no self-respecting non-ego would ever live in—the world of time and space. Everything inside of us and outside of us seems to confirm the belief that we are egos. At this point, the idea would seem totally foolish to question. And hardly anyone ever does.

Yet the fact is, we remain exactly as we were in the beginning. Just as the anorexic stays skinny even though she thinks she is fat, so we remain perfect sons of God, though we think we are egos. We are a heavenly computer; we are simply running the ego program. We are a transcendental slide projector; we are just projecting our infinite light through the dark slide of the ego. We are the perfect Divine actor; we are simply playing the character of the ego in the very long-running play of the separation. The role is nothing, but the actor is everything. "The idols are nothing, but their worshippers are the Sons of God in sickness" (T-10.III.1:8).

In other words, the "you" that thinks you are a human being isn't. The very "you" that thinks you are an intelligent biological organism is really a perfect, untainted piece of Divinity. And this means *you*, not some other part of you. When the Workbook has you say, "I am as God created me" (W-pI.94), it is not talking about some distant or hidden part of you, some higher element buried in your unconscious or reposing in some far-away Heaven. It is talking about the very "you" that is reading these lines, the "you" that is directing your eyes over the page, the "you" whose mind is interpreting these words. Though you cannot see yourself, though everything around you and within you seems to say otherwise, *you* are still as God created you, "You are the holy Son of God Himself" (W-pI.191.6:1).

How Can it Be That I Am Not Inside My Body?

It is one of the most basic, seemingly irrefutable facts of life that we are inside of our bodies. More specifically, we seem to be inside of our heads. And even more specifically, we are right behind our two eyes. In our experience, it seems almost as if we are some kind of spirit or ghost, the "ghost in the machine," trapped inside the body, diffused throughout it, yet focused in the head, mostly the forehead. We assume that the reason we are in the head is because that, in fact, is where the brain is. And inside of the brain is the mind, or so we assume.

Yet from the standpoint of the Course, we are not in our bodies: "The Christ in you inhabits not a body. Yet He is in you. And thus it must be that you are not within a body" (T-25.In.1:1-3). For if we are actually physically located inside of the body and its brain, then we are not Sons of God. For God does not father the limited. What contains you defines you. If the body's walls contain you, then they have power over you, power to define your nature as something limited. And that grants the body power that only God possesses. Only God can define your being, and He does not define you as limited.

How can it possibly be that I am not in my body? As weird as this may sound, it is absolutely possible to give you the experience of being somewhere you are not.

For instance, imagine right now that scientists could shut down your senses entirely, so that you could no longer see, hear, smell, taste, or even feel your body. Imagine also that they shut down your muscles, so that you could not move. And then imagine that they somehow managed to hook up your sensorimotor functions to a Barbie doll, so that you could see out of her eyes, hear out of her ears, and even move her cute little arms and legs. Just imagine for two seconds seeing out of her long-lashed eyes. Without question, I think, you would experience yourself as being located inside of that doll, even though (according to normal thinking) you would still be in your own body.

Obviously, we do not have the technology to carry out the above thought experiment. But we do have the technology to verify its basic point. That technology is called *virtual reality*, a computer technology in which you don a helmet and gloves and actually experience yourself inside a computer-generated environment. As you move your head, the computer scene you see on the inside of the helmet moves accordingly. And as you move your gloved hands you can actually influence and interact with this environment. The point I want to make is that in this computer environment you have a computer-generated body. And it is *this* body, not your "real" body, that you experience yourself being inside of as long as the helmet and gloves are on.

Yet we do not even need highly developed technology to verify this point. We do it every night, *every single night*. Though it has taken very sophisticated technology to give us virtual reality, the mind is an old pro at this process. It does it in its sleep! Every night in our dreams we experience ourselves in a body. And even though this body may seem like our "real" body, it obviously isn't. It is simply an image in our minds. And so, while we are actually (according to normal thinking) inside of our "real" body in bed, we experience ourselves being inside a body-image that is actually inside of our minds!

Based on these three examples I think it is safe to say that the fact that we experience ourselves inside a particular body does not mean much of anything. It certainly does not mean that we are actually in that body. I suggest that we would experience ourselves as being inside *literally anything* our sensorimotor functions were hooked up to—anything whose eyes we could see out of and whose limbs we could move. Given that, we have no good reason for thinking we are inside the body we call our own. There is no reason for thinking it is ultimately any different than the dream body, the virtual reality body, or the Barbie doll.

How Can it Be That I Am Not Inside the World?

Obviously, the issue of not really being inside the world is the same basic issue as not being inside the body. For once we experience ourselves being inside a body, we will experience ourselves being inside whatever environment that body is in. Just as with virtual reality, whatever world that body can see with its eyes, touch with its hands, and move through with its legs, we will have the very convincing experience of being located inside.

What is the physical world, then? I think it is quite safe to say that from the Course's standpoint, this world is simply a collection of images inside our minds. All of its objects are simply mental images held in place by our minds (in cooperation with all other separated minds). All of its events are nothing more than our minds (and all the rest of those minds) moving the images around inside of our minds (see Diagram 5A). Yet we dream all this up from an unconscious place, to hide from ourselves the fact that we are the dreamer. And then we take one particular image, the body-image, and imagine that we are inside of it, that we can see the other images only through its eyes and move the other images only with its limbs (see Diagram 5B). This simple formula, I believe, completely explains the rudiments of our experience in this world. It explains how we can have the very convincing experience of being inside a world that is actually inside our minds.

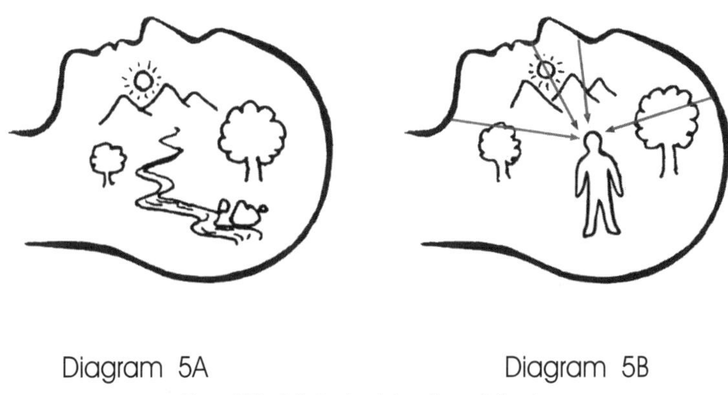

Diagram 5A　　　　Diagram 5B

The World Is Inside the Mind

Therefore, as we run around inside this world, we are running around inside of our own minds. As you walk through your house, for instance, you are walking through your mind. As you drive down the street, you are taking a tour through your own mind. The space "out there" in which everything exists, then, must simply be your own mental space, your own awareness. And all the images you see—the buildings, the cars, the hills, the clouds—are merely the furniture of your own mind, the images of your own mental landscape. It all looks so real and solid because it is all seen through the viewing apparatus of another mental image, the body-image.

It may seem difficult to believe that the entire world exists inside of our minds. Most of us have never imagined that our minds could be anywhere near that big. Yet who is to say that they cannot be? In his

Autobiography of a Yogi, the contemporary Indian saint, Yogananda, records an experience in which this is exactly what he saw:

> People on distant streets seemed to be moving gently over my own remote periphery....A swelling glory within me began to envelop towns, continents, the earth, solar and stellar systems, tenuous nebulae, and floating universes. The entire cosmos, gently luminous, like a city seen afar at night, glimmered within the infinitude of my being.

As you may have noticed, the analogy of nighttime dreaming describes perfectly what I am trying to say about our whole experience here. It is the perfect analogy. It says it all. Here, just as in our nighttime dreams, we seem to be in an imaginary environment that is really inside of our minds. Just as at night, we move through this environment in a dream body that is simply a mental image. Just as at night, the things we do are not really done and have no effect on waking reality. And just as we can sometimes dream we are someone else, so in our daytime dream (our "day-mare" as a friend of mine put it), the person we dream of being has nothing in common with who we—the dreamer—really are. This life, then, is literally a dream. None of it is real. It is all imaginary, it is all inside of our minds.

There is one more crucial element. At night, while you think you are inside of the dream, you are really lying in bed, in your bedroom, at home. Where, then, are you now, while you dream the dream of this world? Where are you lying asleep? And in what bed? Where is your home? We have referred to the Course's answer already many times. It is startling, yet inevitable: "You are at home in God, dreaming of exile" (T-10.I.2:1); "You travel but in dreams, while safe at home" (T-13.VII.17:7). God is your home, your bedroom, your bed and your pillow. My favorite expression of this in the Course is the following:

> You cannot be anywhere God did not put you, and God created you as part of Him. That is both where you are and what you are. It is completely unalterable. It is total inclusion. You cannot change it now or ever. It is forever true. It is not a belief, but a Fact. (T-6.II.6:2-7)

What a wonderful line: "That is both where you are and what you are." It says that the single idea of being "part of God" says everything there is to say about you. It is not simply a statement of *what* you are.

It also identifies *where* you are. You are inside of God, immersed in God, floating in an ocean of God. In other words, you—the very you that thinks you are here—are lying asleep in Heaven, right now, this very instant, where you have always been.

How Can it Be That I Am Not Passing Through Time?

All of the above correctly affirms that we are really the perfect Son of God in Heaven, dreaming we are someone else and somewhere else. Yet it falsely implies that there is an actual passage of time while we dream. It implies that the dream is composed of a linear sequence of moments, one after the other, that together add up to a duration of time.

This, the Course tells us, is false. No time has passed in Heaven while we have been dreaming. The reason should be obvious: there is no time in Heaven! There is only the single Eternal Now, "the endless present, where past and future cannot be conceived" (W-pI.169.6:3). Because there is no time, the Course says that the separation *took* no time. The whole thing, the apparent billions of years of separation, occupied only a "tiny tick of time" (T-26.V.3:5), which "passed away in Heaven too soon for anything to notice it had come" (T-26.V.5:1).

This tiny tick was simply a fragment of eternity perceived as if it were separate, as if it were "splintered from the whole" (T-18.VIII.2:6). The tiny tick was single. It contained no sequence of events. It was a single moment of uniform sleep. Yet, being caused by the thought of fragmentation, it had to keep fragmenting, becoming "so splintered and subdivided and divided again, over and over, that it is now almost impossible to perceive it once was one, and still is what it was" (T-18.I.4:3). The tiny tick seemed to be broken into billions of pieces, "into days and months and years" (T-28.III.7:4). These pieces were not *really* different moments. They were simply different perceptions of the tiny tick, different variations on the theme of sleep. It was as if we stepped into a hall of mirrors and saw the tiny tick multiplied innumerable times from every conceivable angle.

And then, like Scrabble tiles, we mentally arranged these countless fragments into a linear sequence, a gently sloping U-shaped progression in which we gradually fell away from the awakened state and into progressively deeper sleep, and then gradually ascended out of sleep back toward wakefulness. And finally, we then imagined ourselves slowly plodding through this progression one moment at a time, from beginning to end. We had successfully produced the experience of time (see Diagram 6).

Yet, of course, none of this was true. What really happened is that the tiny tick flashed by in Heaven and was over. Since then we have simply been standing outside of time, as we always were, imagining that we are crawling through the shattered fragments of the tiny tick one-by-one, "reviewing mentally what has gone by" (W-pI.158.4:5).

What I find fascinating is that the whole dream, the complete drama of separation, is always in our minds as a whole all at once. The illusion of time is produced by the fact that in each apparently different moment, we are just focusing in on one tiny part of the whole story and simultaneously denying our knowledge of the rest of the story. It would be as if you were mentally reviewing a story you knew by heart, but were imagining that you really didn't know what was going to happen next. This is all that history is. Nothing is really happening. We are outside of time in the single Eternal Now, simply chasing around in our own minds.

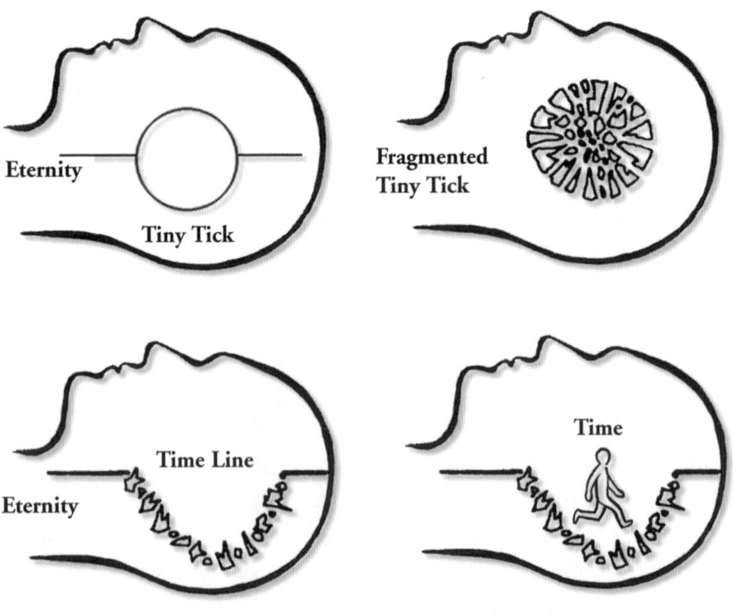

Diagram 6

Time: An Illusion Conjured Within the Mind

The really incomprehensible part is that this "chasing around" is not taking any time. Somehow, in a way we are unable to currently comprehend, the mind is producing the illusion of time while existing in only one single moment, a moment in which there is no time for anything to happen, no time to move our focus from one part of the story to another. I cannot understand how it does this, but I sense that it must be some kind of cosmic psychological shell game, in which the mind simply hides parts of itself from other parts. As the Course says, "Time is a trick, a sleight of hand" (W-pI.158.4:1). Obviously, in trying to understand this, our minds are ranging in realms beyond their comprehension. The Course tells us quite plainly that we cannot understand this. And therefore, thankfully, we do not have to: "And so you are not asked to understand the lack of sequence really found in time" (W-pI.194.4:4).

The point of all this, though, is that nothing has changed. It has not really been fifteen billion years since we separated. No time has passed at all. And so we are just as pure, holy and immaculate as the moment of our birth from the Mind of God. For we are still inside that first moment, since it is the only moment there is, was or ever will be.

Summary

I hope you have caught some glimpse of what this chapter is trying to say: that we can have the very palpable experience of being an individual ego contained within a body, living in the world of space and passing through time, *without any of that being true in the slightest.* The mind is an incredible chameleon. It can give itself the experience of whatever it believes is true. It can experience itself being another person living in another place and another time. It all can seem completely real without any of it actually *being* real. The Son of God is perfectly able to "stand upon a distant shore, and dream himself across an ocean, to a place and time that have long since gone by" (T-26.V.6:6). And that is exactly what we have done. We are not these people, we are not inside these bodies, we do not live in this world, and we do not exist in time. We never have and we never will.

Chapter 10

The Central Paradox

The question that most Course students raise almost right off the bat is "How could the separation have ever occurred?" This is one of the most vexing questions, one that is rendered even more frustrating by the fact that, at least to my mind, it is unsolvable. But before we get into that, let us look at the Course's answers. I am aware of two answers that it gives. Here is the first:

> It is reasonable to ask how the mind could ever have made the ego. In fact, it is the best question you could ask. There is, however, no point in giving an answer in terms of the past because the past does not matter, and history would not exist if the same errors were not being repeated in the present....
>
> Your own state of mind is a good example of how the ego was made. When you threw knowledge away it is as if you never had it. This is so apparent that one need only recognize it to see that it does happen. If this occurs in the present, why is it surprising that it occurred in the past? (T-4.II.1:1-3, 3:1-4)

The gist of this answer is that the same mind that made the ego initially is in the act of remaking it in every second. These current repetitions not only explain how we were capable of making it in the first place, they also are where we should put our focus. For it is only in the present that we can choose differently. We can do nothing about the past.

Whereas the Course's first answer is more pragmatic, its second answer is more philosophical:

> The ego will demand many answers that this course does not give. It does not recognize as questions the mere form of a question to which an answer is impossible. The ego may ask, "How did the impossible occur?", "To what did the impossible happen?", and may ask this in many forms. Yet there is no answer; only an experience. Seek only this, and do not let theology delay you. (C-In.4)

> Who asks you to define the ego and explain how it arose can be but he who thinks it real, and seeks by definition to ensure that its illusive nature is concealed behind the words that seem to make it so.
>
> There is no definition for a lie that serves to make it true. (C-2.2:5-3:1)

The gist of this answer is that the very question is a false question: "How did what could never happen actually happen?" Besides being nonsensical, the question obviously assumes the separation happened. And, as the second passage says, it is designed to. The desire to make the separation real is the actual motivation behind the "question."

Is Our Sleep Real?

Yet it surely seems like something happened, even according to the words of the Course. True, we did not physically detach ourselves from Heaven. We merely dreamt that we did. But doesn't the fact that we are dreaming mean that something happened? Granted: the things we dream about are not real. But we are really dreaming, aren't we? We have actually fallen asleep, right?

On the face of it, the answer would seem to be "yes." The Course says quite clearly that we have not separated from God, we have not changed our nature. But we *have* fallen asleep. "You have chosen a sleep in which you have had bad dreams" (T-6.IV.6:3). We are told plainly, "What He [God] created can sleep, but cannot die"

(T-11.I.9:8). And God is aware of this sleep. He was aware that we were not extending His Love, "So He thought, 'My children sleep and must be awakened'" (T-6.V.1:8). God's awareness of our sleep resulted in two things: 1) In some inscrutable sense, God experienced loneliness (T-4.VII.6:7); and 2) He created the Holy Spirit to wake us up (as the Course states or implies nearly countless times). God created a whole new third Person of the Trinity to clean this problem up. Something definitely seems to have happened.

Apart from all these theological statements in the Course, there is the simple fact of our experience. We do experience the dream. We do feel the pain, the sensations, the emotions, the doubt, the fear, the guilt, the loneliness. And we *are* real. The world we dream of is not, but we are. "*I am real because the world is not*" (W-pI.132.15:3). Therefore, if a real part of Heaven is experiencing this dream, then something has *really* happened.

Yet, on the other hand, how could we have *really* fallen asleep? If our sleep was real, it would be eternal. And for certain lights in Heaven to go dark forever would shatter the integrity of Heaven. Our sleep, then, cannot be real: "You have chosen a sleep...but the sleep is not real" (T-6.IV.6:3). Further, wakefulness is part of our nature, and our nature cannot be changed. There is a very profound discussion of this in Workbook Lesson 167, which in part says, "The mind can think it sleeps, but that is all. It cannot change what is its waking state....[Mind cannot] change its own eternal, mindful state" (W-pI.167.6:1,2,5).

The Course seems to be saying two contradictory things here: 1) The mind has fallen asleep; and 2) It is impossible for mind to fall asleep. How do we resolve this? The only resolution for this that I know is based on the following passage:

> The mind that sees illusions thinks them real. They have existence in that they are thoughts. And yet they are not real, because the mind that thinks these thoughts is separate from God. (W-pI.99.3:2-4)

To apply this to our topic of sleep: Our sleep *exists* but is not *real* ("existence" in this context having a weaker connotation than "reality"). This is obviously a paradox. I just do not think there is any way for our minds to resolve it. And this is not the only example of this paradox.

The Nature of the Mind

We find the exact same paradox when we explore the nature of the little "m" mind. The Course seems to say two very different things about the mind we currently have, the mind that appears to be separate.

One thing the Course clearly says is that the mind we now have is a fragment of our heavenly mind that only seems to have been separated off. The idea of separation "draws a circle, infinitely small, around a very little segment of Heaven" (T-18.VIII.2:6); "around a little part of a glorious and complete idea" (T-18.VIII.2:5). These quotes are from "The Little Garden" section, which also speaks of our mind as a ripple on the ocean of our Self, as a sunbeam off the sun of our Self. Obviously, our separated mind is actually a tiny part of the Christ Mind, a part of God: "Your mind...is part of God" (T-5.VI.7:3); "You are holy because your mind is part of God's" (W-pI.36.1:2).

Thus, the mind is not the ego. The ego is an illusory idea; the mind is a real part of God. The ego-illusion is simply a belief that part of the real mind has adopted about itself. That is why, instead of talking about the ego and the mind as being the same thing, the Course speaks of "the part of the mind the ego rules" (T-4.III.10:1), and "The part of your mind that you have given to the ego [a part of mind we are told will not disappear when the ego does, but] will merely return to the Kingdom, where your whole mind belongs" (T-5.VI.9:5).

Yet it is not quite so simple as this. For the Course in other places more or less equates the ego with the separated mind: "The ego is the part of the mind that believes in division" (T-5.V.3:1); "The ego is the part of the mind that believes your existence is defined by separation" (T-4.VII.1:5).

So according to these references, the ego is actually the part of the mind that believes in the ego. As a result, this part of your mind is an illusion. Several times we are told that only the higher part of our minds is real. And that "The other part of the mind is entirely illusory and makes only illusions" (C-1.4:1); "The other part is a wild illusion, frantic and distraught, but without reality of any kind" (W-pI.49.2:3).

So what is the story here? Is the mind a real part of the Christ Mind that seems separate but is really part of the All? Or is it a thing of the ego that is completely illusory? The Course is saying two different things. What do we do with this? It seems to me that we must believe that *both* are somehow true. The little "m" mind, it seems, is some kind of weird hybrid of ego and Christ, of vacuous illusion and eternal reality. And the Course talks like this. It says:

> The mind is naturally abstract. Part of the mind becomes concrete, however, when it splits. The concrete part believes in the ego, because the ego depends on the concrete. (T-4.VII.1:2-4)

> Complete abstraction is the natural condition of the mind. But part of it is now unnatural. It does not look on everything as one. It sees instead but fragments of the whole, for only thus could it invent the partial world you see. (W-pI.161.2:1-4)

These passages assume that a part of the natively abstract mind actually *becomes* concrete, a part of the natural mind actually *becomes* unnatural, a part of the formless mind *becomes* formed. Based on passages such as these, and on the total collection of references to the mind, the impression I get is the following: Mind itself is formless, changeless, boundless, perfect. Form, change, and attack are all completely outside of its nature. However, when part of the total mind adopts the ego-belief, that part tries to conform itself to the belief. As a result, the ego-belief seems to actually transform this part, pulling it away from the rest, almost like taking a little hunk of clay off of a larger mass of clay. The ego-belief then seems to mold this clay into a particular shape, a shape filled with different sectors, internal conflict, and the constant undulation of change, "a self divided into many warring parts, separate from God, and tenuously held together by its erratic and capricious maker [the ego]" (W-pI.95.2:2). The resulting little mind is an interesting creature:

1. The substance of this little mind—what it is made of—is still the clay, the substance of eternal mind. As a result, its native desires are for mind's true condition. It cannot truly desire anything but God's Love. That is why it is only able to extend love or call for love. Further, its abilities are simply smaller versions of mind's true abilities (T-3.IV.1:1;T-3.V.1:1). Its ability to think, choose, feel, be aware, project, and extend, are tiny drops from the ocean of its true power to create, to know, and to love. In other words, both the desires and abilities of this little mind point to the fact that it is made of the substance of eternal mind.

2. This substance of eternal mind, though, has somehow been molded into a form, the form of the ego. The little mind's form, then, *is* the ego, and so includes separation, limitation, change, conflict, and attack.
3. There is thus a very direct conflict between the substance and the form of this little mind. The form contradicts the substance, since the substance is formless. The little mind is thus a hybrid composed of totally conflicting elements.
4. The little mind will experience this conflict as pain. For its nature is being violated by the form it is in, like a wild animal that is put in a cage. And so the fundamental condition of the little mind will be one of suffering.
5. Yet, its substance—that of eternal mind—cannot really be violated. You cannot mold the inherently shapeless. There is no such thing as formed formlessness. Thus there can be no real hybrid. And since the little mind *is* a hybrid, it must be an illusion.

Perhaps a better metaphor, then, will be to envision the mind as a mirror: pure, flawless, and changeless. What the ego does is seemingly produce a bubble on the surface of the mirror, a bubble that, though pulled from the mirror, is quite different than the mirror itself. It is a contortion of the mirror, a metamorphosis of part of it. The bubble, though made of the pure, transparent glass of the mirror, is an opaque swirling mass of change, division, and conflict. Because the form of this bubble is a violation of its substance (the glass), this bubble will be in constant pain. Yet because of this same violation, the bubble cannot be real. Mirrors cannot have bubbles. And so the bubble must be nothing more than an illusory image in the mirror, a mere reflection. The image of the bubble, with all of its swirling change and conflict, passes across the mirror, yet the mirror remains the same, serenely unaffected by this fleeting image.

Now if you are having problems really grasping this idea, good. I can't grasp it either. And that is the point: it is a paradox. Clearly, if we read everything the Course has to say about the little "m" mind, we come up with a paradox. Our current mind is both illusory form and real substance. It is, as I said, a weird hybrid. It *exists*, but is *not real*.

The Central Paradox

In examining the reality of our sleep and exploring the nature of the separated mind,as we have seen, we come smack up against the exact same paradox. Just as our sleep exists but is not real, so our sleeping mind exists but is not real. In other words, they are really not separate topics at all. Both are answers to the same question: Can transcendental mind enter into a different state of mind than its natural formless, changeless, fully awake condition? And the answer, again, is "yes" and "no," or "emphatically no," but "kind of." Our sleeping state and sleeping mind *exist* but are *not real.*

I think that this paradox is unresolvable from our current state of mind. I think we just have to live with it. It is uncomfortable, true. But we have to just sit on it, nonetheless. It is, I believe, the central paradox of the Course. The whole Course revolves around this single ungraspable paradox. And thus we must just leave it be, for if we try to resolve it toward either side, we have to rewrite the entire Course, and, worse than that, shatter its hopeful message of salvation.

If we try to resolve it toward the heavenly side, saying that our sleep is not real and *does not even exist*, the consequences are major. In this scenario, God could not have seen us fall asleep, and therefore could not have created the Holy Spirit to wake us up. And since we cannot wake up on our own, we are now in big trouble. Yet, in this scenario, why should our waking up be important? Given that our sleeping minds are pure and absolute illusions, who cares if they wake up or not? Why even try? Let's just break out the booze and have a ball.

If we try to resolve the paradox toward the earthly side, saying that our sleep both exists *and is real*, the trouble is just as serious, even more so. For then what God created really can change its original wakeful condition. We really have changed our nature from waking to sleeping, from formless to formed. And we are doomed, since what is real is eternal. We will always be this way. Again, who's got the booze?

And so, uncomfortable or not, I think we just have to live with this paradox. And why not? Why should we assume that such things can be grasped by our separated minds? If we could answer the question of the separation with our separated minds, then those minds would be able to grasp reality itself. For the question we are asking is really a question about reality. We are, in essence, asking the reality-status of the separation. In other words, what does the separation look like from the perspective of reality? And if our minds could grasp how *anything* looks from the perspective of reality, then reality would not transcend our current condition, but would be on par with it. It would be just another boring thing of time and space.

I think that the Course refers to the unresolvable nature of the question when it says, "Yet there is no answer; only an experience. Seek only this, and do not let theology delay you" (C-In.4:4-5). When it says, "there is no answer; only an experience," I take that to mean, "there is no answer as you understand answers. It can only be understood from within the experience of reality."

You may have noticed that this paradox is in essence the same basic paradox that we discussed in Part I. There we saw that Heaven is pure oneness, but that within that unity was somehow contained a trace of diversity. Here in Part II we see that Heaven is pure wakefulness, but that within that waking is somehow contained a trace of sleep. As you can see, both are more or less the same paradox. And therefore they must have more or less the same resolution, a "resolution" which, fortunately or unfortunately, must still lie beyond our current comprehension.

The "resolution" for the paradox of unity and diversity was that somehow—in a manner beyond our grasp—Heaven can contain a trace of diversity without in the least compromising its fundamental unity. In Part I we reviewed a passage that spoke of this (T-3.IV.1:5-8). It said, in essence, that even though the idea of levels seems to necessarily imply distinction, boundaries, separation, the Levels of the Trinity are capable of perfect unity. Somehow Heaven can contain diversity without compromising its unity.

The same must be true for the paradox of wakefulness and sleep. Somehow Heaven can contain a faint trace of sleep without in the least compromising its fundamental wakefulness. Somehow Heaven can include a sleep which exists without being real, without at all violating Heaven's fundamental waking condition.

The Tiny Separation

I think that somehow the key here is that the diversity and the sleep are truly nothing more than faint traces, vastly overshadowed by the infinite magnitude of Heaven's oneness/wakefulness. Otherwise it would not be a paradox that we could expect to resolve when our minds go beyond questioning to the naked truth. It would simply be a hopeless contradiction. For the paradox to have any hope of ultimate resolution, one side of it must be minimal, the other side maximal. And this is the exact situation we find in the Course. This is why the Course is always using the word "tiny" in speaking of the ego and the separation, talking about the ego as a "tiny mouse," about the "tiny, mad idea" that the separation really is, about the "tiny segment" of our minds that dream of it, and about the "tiny tick of time" in which it seemed to occur.

In other words, the Course minimizes the side of the paradox which says our sleep exists. It minimizes our sleep first by asserting that the part of our minds that fell asleep was "a little corner" (W-pI.190.6:6), a microscopic piece, an infinitesimal splinter:

> This fragment of your mind is such a tiny part of it that, could you but appreciate the whole, you would see instantly that it is like the smallest sunbeam to the sun, or like the faintest ripple on the surface of the ocean. (T-18.VIII.3:3)

It also minimizes our sleep by asserting that, as we saw in the last chapter, all of time took place in one "tiny tick," and that this tick is *already over*, having been instantly corrected by God: "What God gave answer to is answered and is gone" (T-26.V.3:7). Imagine that: all of time already happened and we are now standing outside of it, simply "reviewing mentally what has gone by" (W-pI.158.4:5). Time, then, was tiny and is over. In short, time was an exceedingly insignificant event. It "passed away in Heaven too soon for anything to notice it had come...too quickly to affect the simple knowledge of the Son of God" (T-26.V.5:1-2).

In summary: our life, our memories, our past lives, and any experiences in other dimensions besides this earth; indeed, our entire passage through time and space, spanning some billions of years, as well as the universe of time and space itself, and any other dream universes and planes that seem to exist; *all of it is a minute dream in a microscopic fragment of our minds that lasted only a tiny instant and is already over.* And even the brief, tiny flash of sleep in which this dream occurred was not real. It only *seemed* to happen. "[The mind] merely seems to go to sleep a while....When the mind awakes, it but continues as it always was" (W-pI.167.9:2,4).

Chapter 11

The Message of *A Course In Miracles*

We have examined a great many very abstract philosophical issues in both Parts I and II, from the nature of God, Christ, and ourselves, to the origin, nature, and purpose of the world. By this point you may be wondering what the relevance is of all these abstract ideas. What is their practical value? What good do they do us?

You may also be depressed by many of the ideas that have been presented here in Part II. It can be depressing enough to be told that the world is an illusion, let alone to be told that it is a dream being dreamt in our own minds apart from God, a dream that is a psychological defense against Divine reality and an outpicturing of our attack on God and our attraction to guilt.

Yet the ideas we have explored are neither irrelevant nor ultimately depressing. Far from it. The Course's idea that the separation was not real but purely psychological, occurring strictly in the privacy of our minds, yields results that are inspiring, even exhilarating. They provide a profound and liberating answer to the most crucial question there is: How do we surmount the barriers to ultimate happiness?

In this world there seem to be so many things standing between us and happiness. Our happiness seems to lie outside of us, in outer events, conditions, objects, and people. We need to earn money, buy possessions, acquire status, chase honors, and win friends and lovers. Yet the world is loath to give us these things. It yields up its treasures with extreme reluctance. It has its own will and its own needs. It does not jump with the snap of our fingers (unless, of course, there is money in those fingers).

A big part of winning the world's favor and earning our own peace of mind is in improving ourselves, becoming a better person, however we define that. It seems that we need to acquire skills and develop talents; become more knowledgeable, learned and cultured; learn how to communicate better; become more kind and generous; become more aggressive and confident; make our body stronger, healthier and more attractive; and the list goes on. Yet just as the world does not instantly respond to our will, our own self is just as recalcitrant, perhaps even more. For we are the product of our past, of our heredity and environment. And that past has locked us into certain hardened patterns. Further, that past has loaded us with debts to pay. If we are to have peace and happiness, our past sins need to be paid off. This is one barrier to happiness that is very painful to surmount.

These barriers, both within and without, are so large, solid, and high that life can seem like running the million-meter hurdles, with each hurdle being a fifteen-foot concrete barrier. As soon as you have—God knows how—made it over one hurdle, right in the middle of congratulating yourself you are immediately faced with the next. And so you scale that one hoping that it is the last, until you are over it and see that it isn't. And all the while you hope against hope that you are not penalized and brought back to the beginning.

Because the barriers to happiness in this world are seemingly so many and so solid, real happiness seems distant in time. Apparently, it must be won over many, many years of hard work. Yet for most people, even after all that work, things don't seem to get all that much better. They may even get worse.

What do we do about these limits to happiness? What do we do about the fact that we are surrounded by things that limit us and hurt us, things that just do not go away? Our bodies, our minds, our personalities, our pasts, our lives, our society, our world, and even space and time themselves, all seem to pen us in, to imprison us and punish us, keeping us ever separate from the elusive treasure of ultimate happiness. What can we do about this?

Reality and Illusion

The Course's answer to this question lies in the nature of reality and the nature of illusion. Reality, as we saw in Part I, is a realm that is perfect. It is "not a place nor a condition. It is merely an awareness of perfect oneness, and the knowledge that there is nothing else; nothing outside this oneness and nothing else within" (T-18.VI.1:5-6). It contains no suffering whatsoever. There are no limits, no barriers, no boundaries of any kind. There exists only limitless love and eternal peace. This realm is not just real, it is the only reality. It is reality itself.

Therefore, anything else, anything apart from this perfect oneness, is not real. Anything painful, lacking, limited, unstable, uncertain, partial, or impermanent is an illusion. Anything even remotely confining or sorrowful, even slightly less than the Infinite, is unreal. And unreal means unreal. Illusions are "Nothingness, but in a form that seems like something" (C-2.2:2). Illusions have no objective reality whatsoever. They only seem real in our minds.

Yet because they are in our minds alone, the power to change them is ours. All the limitations and flaws within us, and all the powerful, unfriendly forces outside of us, are just pictures of our beliefs, beliefs that are only in our minds. We are the ones that produced them, and our active maintenance is the only thing that keeps them going. If we simply stop supporting them, they will be gone, instantly and without a trace.

Illusions, then, are the precise opposite of what the world makes them seem. In Chapter 7 we saw that we made the world in order that the idea of separation could seem to be an objective reality that had power over us, rather than our own idea that we could change. In actuality it is the exact reverse. The idea of separation—and all that goes with it—is nothing but an idea in our minds. It has no reality of its own.

In other words, there are no real, objective barriers to happiness. The only barriers are subjective; they only exist in our minds. Infinite happiness is held out to us this instant. All of those fifteen-foot concrete walls standing between us and happiness are our own hallucination. They are not really there. We are already standing past the finishing line, merely hallucinating that we are going over those endless hurdles. We are done. We are there. We are home.

Infinite happiness, of course, is another way of talking about the

Goal of goals, union with God. To appreciate what the Course is saying, let us go one-by-one through the obstacles that seem to lie between us and God.

Separateness

As long as we think we are separate individuals, we will think that God is outside of us, that we are "locked in a separate prison, removed and unreachable, incapable of reaching out as being reached" (T-18.VI.7:5). At best we can think that God left some little spark of Himself buried deep within us. Either way, there seem to be objective barriers to surmount in order to reach total and absolute immersion in God.

Yet, as we saw, we are not really separate from God. We are inside of God. "You are surrounded only by Him. What limits can there be on you whom He encompasses?" (T-18.VI.10:6-7). We have merely fantasized that we are not inside of Him, and we can give up this fantasy any time we choose.

Guilt

According to the Course, guilt is the main thing that keeps our fantasy of separation going. Think about it: if you really believed that you had done all of the things described in this book, your guilt would make the guilt of a Hitler look like nothing. And the fact is, somewhere in your mind you *do* believe all that. Somewhere inside you believe that you have screwed up so bad that you are an eternally lost cause.

Guilt is the belief that we are undeserving of our Father's Love, unworthy of standing in His Presence. Guilt claims that instead of His Love we deserve His wrath, His punishment, His hell. As long as we believe in guilt, then we will automatically exclude ourselves from God. Under this belief, we will do all kinds of somersaults to get back in His good graces. We will try to earn our way out of guilt through being good and holy. We will try to pay for our guilt through self-inflicted punishment of one form or another. Or we will try to believe that Jesus paid for our sins on the cross. Yet all these attempts will be conflicted, being based both on our desire to be with God *and* our belief that we do not deserve to be.

This is one of many places where the Course dramatically parts company with traditional Christianity, which sees the Fall as a real event, causing real guilt and provoking real Divine wrath. In the Course, since there was no real Fall, there is nothing to get mad over and nothing to feel guilty about. Our guilt is merely psychological; it is not real, moral, legal guilt. Leaving our Father's home, blowing it up, and then building our own home out of the fragments—none of this should cause the slightest guilt in us because none of it actually happened. We merely had a dream in which we did bad things. And we have been too ashamed to go home ever since, thinking that our Father's wrath would be waiting for us. We are like the prodigal son: "He was ashamed to return to his father, because he thought he had hurt him. Yet when he came home the father welcomed him with joy, because the son himself *was* his father's treasure. He wanted nothing else" (T-8.VI.4:2-4). This is how our Father waits for us.

> In the temple, Holiness waits quietly for the return of them that love it. The Presence knows they will return to purity and to grace. The graciousness of God will take them gently in, and cover all their sense of pain and loss with the immortal assurance of their Father's Love. (T-14.IX.4:1-3)

The Course gives us this same message, over and over again, speaking to that part of us that remembers our deed, yet never got the news that it had no effects:

> A madman's dreams are frightening, and sin appears indeed to terrify. And yet what sin perceives is but a childish game. The Son of God may play he has become a body, prey to evil and to guilt, with but a little life that ends in death. But all the while his Father shines on him, and loves him with an everlasting Love which his pretenses cannot change at all.
>
> How long, O Son of God, will you maintain the game of sin? Shall we not put away these sharp-edged children's toys? How soon will you be ready to come home? Perhaps today? There is no sin. Creation is unchanged.

> Would you still hold return to Heaven back? How long, O holy Son of God, how long? (W-pII.4.4-5)

Our Imperfect Nature

All of us go around feeling that we are imperfect people, that we must be perfected before we can be with God. This, of course, has everything to do with the above two categories—our separateness and our guilt—but I feel it deserves its own mention.

Because of our assumed imperfection, spiritual systems all over the world have provided ways to become perfect. These ways include training our minds on the Divine within, developing our powers of mind and body, becoming accomplished in good works, overcoming sinful thoughts. In the section, "I Need Do Nothing" (T-18.VIII), the Course itself focuses on two of these ways, what one could call the primary Western stream and the main Eastern stream:

> It is extremely difficult to reach Atonement by fighting against sin. Enormous effort is expended in the attempt to make holy what is hated and despised. Nor is a lifetime of contemplation and long periods of meditation aimed at detachment from the body necessary. All such attempts will ultimately succeed because of their purpose. Yet the means are tedious and very time consuming, for all of them look to the future for release from a state of present unworthiness. (T-18.VII.4:7-11)

In other words, the idea that you have an imperfect nature that needs to be perfected is the idea that you are not worthy of the ultimate reward right now. You have to go through a lengthy perfection process. And this belief is itself what makes it take a long time.

In contrast, the Course affirms that you are worthy of the ultimate reward now, for you are already perfect now. Your personality, the person you think you are, is not perfect. It is ridiculous. But the "you" that thinks you are that personality is a real part of God. You do not need to become holy, mystical, selfless or powerful. You need only open your eyes. And you will find that you already are all of those things, in infinite measure.

The Body

The body is seemingly one of the major concrete barriers to God. Spiritual traditions have acknowledged this for thousands of years. Not only does the body seem to make us separate, as well as blind us to all the glory its senses cannot see, it is an all-consuming involvement. It has constant needs for food, clothing and shelter. And it has powerful desires for physical satisfaction, for the pleasures of taste, comfort, and sex. It leads us around by the nose, making us feel pain when it hurts, feel sick when it's sick and even making us die when it dies. The body's insatiable needs and desires require us to make it our first responsibility, pitting us against everything we see, forcing us to defend it against what would otherwise be friends, compelling us to plunder the world around us to feed its quotas. How can we follow God when our body demands that we make *it* our god?

Yet from the Course's standpoint, the body is simply a mental image, a dream symbol. It has no power over us. We are not inside of it, not now and not ever, any more than we are inside our dream body at night. To escape the body, all we need do is fully realize this. This is why the Workbook has us affirm, over and over, "I am not a body, I am free" (W-pI.199).

> Freedom must be impossible as long as you perceive a body as yourself. The body is a limit. Who would seek for freedom in a body looks for it where it can not be found. The mind can be made free when it no longer sees itself as in a body, firmly tied to it and sheltered by its presence. (W-pI.199.1-4)

The World

The world seems to be an enormous barrier to God. It seems to place us in a different universe than God, a place where He is nowhere to be found. How could we possibly get to a formless Heaven from a physical universe? And while we are trying to figure that one out, the world is constantly at work, from birth to death, sunrise to sunrise, molding and shaping us into a creature of the world, rather than a saint of God. It seems to shove our faces down in the mud, making us appreciate the supreme value of material needs and concerns, making us before anything else put food on the table, clothes on our body, gas in the car. And the people around us, our family, friends, and society, are incessantly indoctrinating us in how to be intelligent animals rather than celestial spirits. Living in the world is like belonging to one big religious cult, where everyone must think according to the unspoken party line. It seems impossible to find God's infinite happiness while living in this world.

Yet the world is no barrier at all between us and God. It is our dream, our psychological construct. We made it up to *look like* a concrete wall between us and God. In truth, "There is no world! This is the central thought the course attempts to teach" (W-pI.132.6:2-3).

Now I hope you can see why the Course is so relentlessly down on this world. For this is a world of limits. It is less than Heaven, to say the least. And any theory that makes it real tacitly affirms its power to limit us. There are many ways to do this. We can say that God produced the world. Or that the world produced itself. Or that the world is evil and must be battled against. Or that the world is good and must be loved and embraced (on a form level). All of these clothe the world of limits in reality and therefore power. And what do you think real and powerful limits do? They limit; they imprison. Therefore, only if the world is an idea that we had apart from God, an idea that exists in our minds alone, can this world have no power over us, no power to cast us in a prison apart from our Eternal Love.

Time

Because of all these apparent barriers between us and God, attaining infinite happiness seems to be a long way off. It seems to be a case of the million-meter hurdles. Time, then, appears to be the final barrier standing between us and God, the net result of all the other barriers.

Yet what if the Course is right? What if there are no real obstacles keeping us from God? If that is true, it is only our belief in obstacles that makes our return to God take time. And the more serious are the obstacles we believe in, the more time it takes.

To clarify this, let us use an analogy. Let's say we have three people and we give them all the task of walking from one end of a room to the other as quickly as they can. Yet two of these people we hypnotize. In one of their minds we plant the suggestion that between him and the other end of the room are all kinds of closed, locked doors and in between those doors is furniture piled to the ceiling. In the mind of the other we plant the suggestion that there are merely several large piles of children's toys in the way (which in my house it would not take a hypnotist to convince one of). The third person we leave un-hypnotized. The result is a foregone conclusion. You already know who will get to the other side of the room first, second and last.

This analogy tells us everything about the spiritual process. For all of us are hypnotized into thinking there is distance to go, when in fact we are already standing at the end: "The journey to God is merely the reawakening of the knowledge of where you are always and what you are forever. It is a journey without distance to a goal that has never changed" (T-8.VI.9:6-7). The awakening process, then, is an illusion. Just as we never really left God in the first place, so it only seems to us that we progressively approach God, becoming more and more deserving of His Love. In actuality, spiritual progress means simply shedding the fear of the gift that was held out to us at every moment along the way. In other words, awakening does not have to take any time. It only takes as long as we *think* it has to. If we think that God is earned only after eons of arduous spiritual labor, eons it will take. Yet the ironic thing is that even after all of that work, when we at last awaken, we will realize, in one shattering glimpse, that the gift was ours all along:

> When peace comes at last to those who wrestle with temptation and fight against the giving in to sin; when the light comes at last into the mind given to contemplation; or when the goal is finally achieved by anyone, it always comes with just one happy realization; "*I need do nothing.*" (T-18.VII.5:7)

The Course is trying to save us this time. It has formed a path which in all its parts is nothing but a constant rehearsal of the fact that the gift is ours at every moment.

> The emphasis of this course always remains the same;—it is at this moment that complete salvation is offered you, and it is at this moment that you can accept it. (M-24.6:1)

The hope, then, is that if all we do is practice different forms of this single thought, then we will "slip past centuries of effort, and escape from time" (T-18.VII.7:3). If all we do is practice the fact that we and everyone else are still the perfect Sons of God, still at rest within the Heart of God; if all we do is look straight at our illusions and remember that no sin is real, that even the ultimate "sin" of "wrecking" God's Kingdom was only a harmless mistake, that God still waits for us with the open Arms of Love; then surely we will hasten the day of awakening.

On that day we will not become the slightest bit holier. We will merely have let go the fear of knowing what is real. And so we will awaken to knowledge which cannot be spoken, yet is more familiar than anything words have ever described. We will open our eyes in the vastness of Heaven and realize we never left, and slept but for a brief second. And God—if His response could possibly be translated into terms our minds can now comprehend—will merely say, "Good morning, My Son."

> All little things are silent. Little sounds are soundless now. The little things of earth have disappeared. The universe consists of nothing but the Son of God, who calls upon his Father. And his Father's Voice gives answer in his Father's holy Name. In this eternal, still relationship, in which communication far transcends all words, and yet exceeds in depth and height whatever words could possibly convey, is peace eternal. (W-pI.183.11:1-6)

The Circle's Mission Statement

To discern the author's vision of *A Course in Miracles* and manifest that in our lives, in the lives of students, and in the world.

1

To faithfully discern the author's vision of *A Course in Miracles.*

In interpreting the Course we strive for total fidelity to its words and the meanings they express. We thereby seek to discover the Course as the author saw it.

2

To be an instrument in Jesus' plan to manifest his vision of the Course in the lives of students and in the world.

We consider this to be Jesus' organization and therefore we attempt to follow his guidance in all we do. Our goal is to help students understand, as well as discern for them selves, the Course's thought system as he intended, and use it as he meant it to be used—as a literal program in spiritual awakening. Through doing so we hope to help ground in the world the intended way of doing the Course, here at the beginning of its history.

3

To help spark an enduring tradition based entirely on students joining together in doing the Course as the author envisioned.

We have a vision of local Course support systems composed of teachers, students, healers, and groups, all there to support one another in making full use of the Course. These support systems, as they continue and multiply, will together comprise an enduring spiritual tradition, dedicated solely to doing the Course as the author intended. Our goal is to help spark this tradition, and to assist others in doing the same.

4

To become an embodiment, a birthplace of this enduring spiritual tradition.

To help spark this tradition we must first become a model for it ourselves. This requires that we at the Circle follow the Course as our individual path; that we ourselves learn forgiveness through its program. It requires that we join with each other in a group holy relationship dedicated to the common goal of awakening through the Course. It also requires that we cultivate a local support system here in Sedona, and that we have a facility where others could join with us in learning this approach to the Course. Through all of this we hope to become a seed for an ongoing spiritual tradition based on *A Course in Miracles*.

Books & Booklets in this Series

Commentaries on *A Course in Miracles* by Robert Perry and Allen Watson

1. **Seeing the Face of Christ in All Our Brothers** *by Perry*. How we can see the Presence of God in others. $5.00

3. **Shrouded Vaults of the Mind** *by Perry*. Draws a map of the mind based on the Course, and takes you on a tour through its many levels. $5.00

4. **Guidance: Living the Inspired Life** *by Perry*. Sketches an overall perspective on guidance and its place on the spiritual path. $7.00

8. **A Healed Mind Does Not Plan** *by Watson*. Examines our approach to planning and decision-making, showing how it is possible to leave the direction of our lives up to the Holy Spirit. $5.00

9. **Through Fear to Love** *by Watson*. Explores two sections from the Course that deal with our fear of redemption. Leads the reader to see how it is possible to look upon ourselves with love. $5.00

10. **The Journey Home** *by Watson*. Presents a description of our spiritual destination and what we must go through to get there. $5.00

11. **Everything You Always Wanted to Know About Judgment but Were Too Busy Doing It to Notice** *by Perry and Watson*. A survey of various teachings about judgment in the Course. $8.00

12. **The Certainty of Salvation** *by Perry and Watson*. How we can become certain that we will find our way to God. $5.00

13. **What is Death?** *by Watson*. The Course's view of what death really is. $5.00

14. **The Workbook as a Spiritual Practice** *by Perry*. A guide for getting the most out of the Workbook. $5.00

15. **I Need Do Nothing: Finding the Quiet Center** *by Watson*. An in-depth discussion of one of the most misunderstood sections of the Course. $5.00

16. **A Course Glossary** *by Perry*. 150 definitions of terms and phrases from the Course for students and study groups. $7.00

17. **Seeing the Bible Differently: How *A Course in Miracles* Views the Bible** *by Watson*. Shows the similarities, differences, and continuity between the Course and the Bible. $6.00

18. **Relationships as a Spiritual Journey: From Specialness to Holiness** *by Perry*. Describes the Course's unique view of how we can find God through the transformation of our relationships. $10.00

19. **A Workbook Companion Volume I** *by Watson and Perry.* Commentaries on Lessons 1 - 120. $16.00

20. **A Workbook Companion Volume II** *by Watson and Perry.* Commentaries on Lessons 121 - 243. $16.00

21. **A Workbook Companion Volume III** *by Watson and Perry.* Commentaries on Lessons 244 - 365. $18.00

22. **The Answer Is a Miracle** *by Perry and Watson*. Looks at what the Course means by miracles, and how we can experience them in our lives. $7.00

23. **Let Me Remember You** *by Perry and Watson*. Regaining a sense of God's relevance, both in the Course and in our lives. $10.00

24. **Bringing the Course to Life: How to Unlock the Meaning of *A Course in Miracles* for Yourself** *by Watson and Perry*. Designed to teach the student, through instruction, example and exercises, how to read the Course so that the experience becomes a personal encounter with the truth. $12.00

25. **Reality and Illusion: An Overview of Course Metaphysics** *by Perry.* Examines the Course's lofty vision of reality, its account of the events which gave birth to our current existence, and how the Course views the relationship between ultimate reality and the illusory world of separation. $11.00

For shipping rates, a complete catalog of our products and services, or for information about events, please contact us at:

The Circle of Atonement
Teaching and Healing Center
P.O. Box 4238
W. Sedona, AZ 86340
(928) 282-0790, Fax (928) 282-0523
E-mail: info@circleofa.com
Website: www.circleofa.com

Read
T 11. VI

Vince
UN-Living ACIM
Pw is, ALIVE #12.

T1-4-V